Thought you
might enjoy
this

Dartmoor

Dartmoor

Exeter   Newton Abbot   Totnes
Plymouth   Teignmouth   Dawlish

Kenneth E. Lowther and Reginald
J. W. Hammond

The section on *Walks and Rides on
Dartmoor* by Brian Le Messurier

WARD LOCK LIMITED · LONDON

© Ward Lock Limited 1979
Published in Great Britain in 1979 by
Ward Lock Limited, 116 Baker Street,
London W1M 2BB, a Pentos Company

Set, printed and bound in Great Britain by
Cox and Wyman Ltd,
London, Fakenham and Reading

British Library Cataloguing in Publication Data

Lowther, Kenneth Ernest
   Dartmoor guide. – (Red guides).
   1. Dartmoor, Eng – Description and travel – Guide-books
   I. Title   II. Hammond, Reginald James William
   III. Le Messurier, Brian   IV. Series
   914.23'53'04857   DA670.D2

ISBN 0–7063–5792–2
ISBN 0–7063–5719–4 Pbk

The pictures were kindly supplied by the following:
Peter Baker Photography: pages 12, 27, 46, 75, 77, 78, 87, 99,
   103, 119, 123; J. Allan Cash: pages 73, 112 lower; British
   Tourist Authority: page 90; A. F. Kersting: pages 45, 82,
   111, 112 upper.

Contents

Walks and Rides on Dartmoor

Maps and Plans

Illustrations

Introduction

Dartmoor is one of the few areas of great beauty in England that have remained largely undeveloped and have retained the secrets of their remoteness. It is a place of quickly changing moods and colours; much of the land is bleak and bare but its valleys, romantic gorges and charming unspoilt villages offer a smiling welcome which attracts thousands of visitors. Those who walk or ride get most out of the Moor, for its countless paths and bridleways offer a multiplicity of routes. Roads are comparatively few but even the motorist can obtain some idea of the area's unique character. It is particularly a paradise for painter and sportsman, for photographer and naturalist.

A good deal of accommodation is available in the villages on the Moor itself and considerably more is to be found in the busy little towns on its borders such as Ashburton and Tavistock. But most of the Moor's visitors travel either from one of Devon's many coastal resorts or from one of the four centres described in detail in this volume—Exeter, Newton Abbot, Totnes and Plymouth.

Exeter, the county capital, is a fine city with a magnificent cathedral and many historic buildings of absorbing interest. It is a convenient centre not only for Dartmoor but for the whole of Devon since roads radiate in every direction to bring coastal and inland areas within an easy day's drive. The prosperous town of Newton Abbot is another excellent touring centre. The medieval town of Totnes, with its old walls and gates, its Norman castle and its Tudor Guildhall, attracts lovers of the past. Plymouth, largely rebuilt since severe bombing in World War II, is the largest city in Devon and is a splendid centre for the coast and nearby Dartmoor.

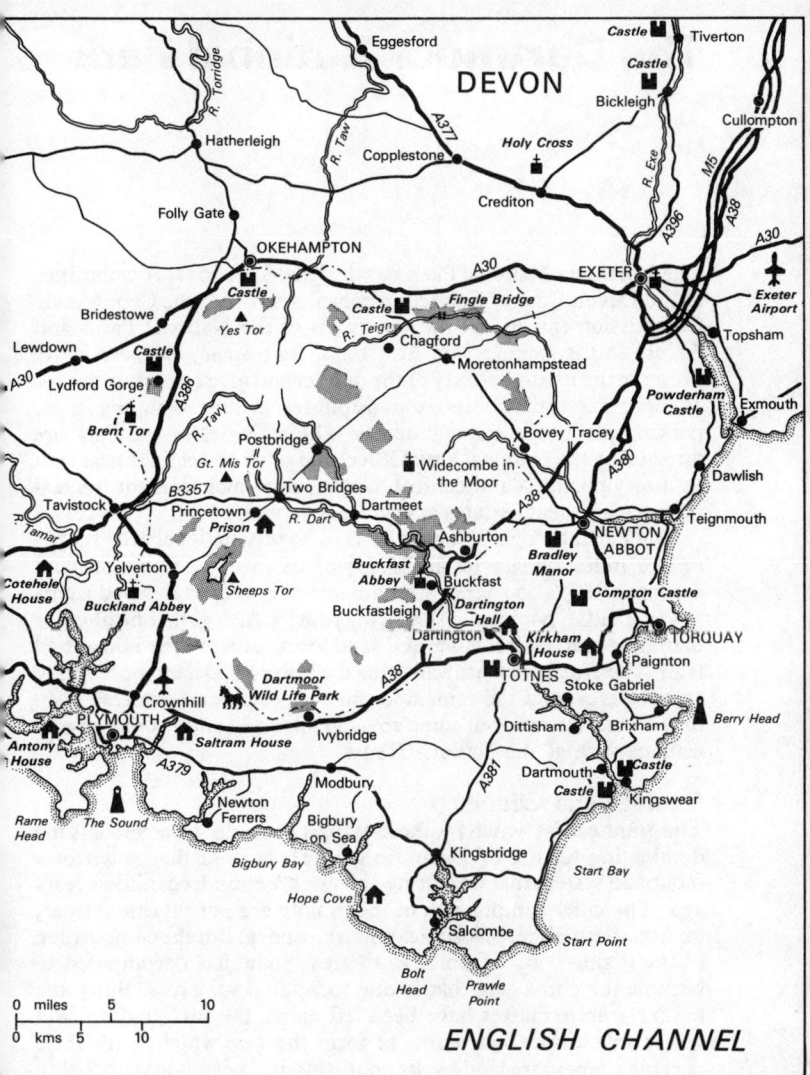

The Dartmoor National Park

The Dartmoor National Park was designated in 1951. A committee of the Devon County Council in consultation with the Countryside Commission carries out the provisions of the National Parks and Access to the Countryside Act, 1949. Its primary purpose is "to preserve the natural beauty of the district and give opportunities for open-air recreation". Its responsibilities include camping sites, parking places and general access. The activities of the Park are directed by the National Park Office, and separate sections deal with statutory planning and control, conservation management, recreation management, estates and visitors services.

The Park, though "National", is in no way nationalized. Its 365 square miles remain in the hands of its owners. Common land accounts for 96,000 acres. Commoners have old-established rights to graze cattle, ponies and sheep, dig peat for fuel, gather heather for thatching, and collect stone and sand for repairs to their homes and land. The Duchy of Cornwall owns the Forest of Dartmoor covering 70,000 acres, and the remainder belongs to private owners. They may be individuals, but some are councils and various other organizations such as the National Trust.

Geology and Climate

The granite mass which for the most part comprises Dartmoor is the dominating feature of Devon in general. It is all that is left of a mountain system that was formed about three hundred million years ago. The chief components of the granite are porphyritic felspar, quartz, tourmaline, black mica and white mica. But the composition of the granite varies from area to area. Some has decomposed to become the china clay that is dug today in some areas. But some harder granite masses have been left above the surrounding land where the surface has worn, to form the tors which, with their varying shapes, are landmarks on the Moor. Igneous activity led to

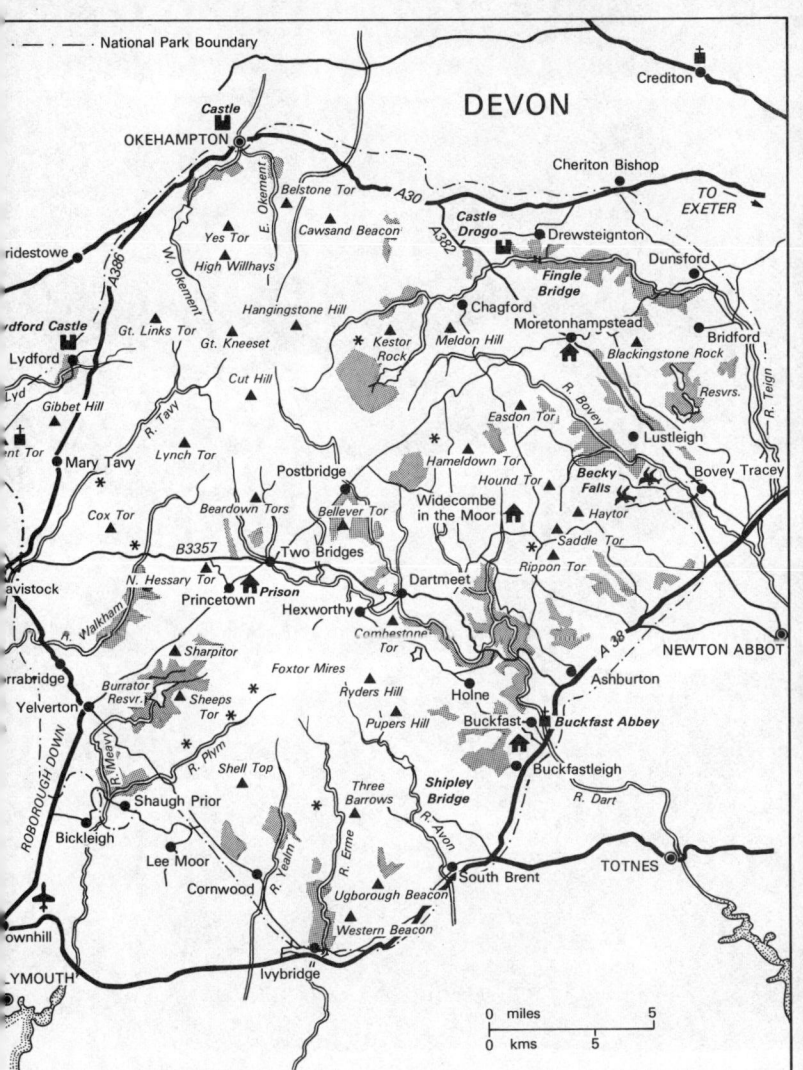

Becky Falls

the formation of lodes of minerals including arsenic, copper, lead, iron, manganese, silver and tin, some of which were worked by miners on a large scale. A great deal of igneous rock is also to be found, particularly on the eastern side where volcanic rock has been quarried for building stones.

Dartmoor is largely a region of rolling uplands on which the granite hills form rounded shapes and gentle slopes. Valleys are generally wide and shallow, rarely steep though there are a few gorges. The highest points are in the north where High Willhays rises to 2,038 feet and Yes Tor to 2,030 feet, but the average elevation of the Moor is 1,200 feet. Only two of its rivers flow to the coast of North Devon; most, including the most important the Dart, flow southwards. The sources of the majority of the rivers are in the northern plateau, but there is also a group comprising the Avon, Erme, Plym and Yealm which rises in the southern part. There are no natural lakes but a number of reservoirs have been constructed.

In general Dartmoor is extremely liable to rain, fogs and mists. Rainfall is heaviest in the region of the western hills. Over a recent twenty-year period the mean annual rainfall recorded at Princetown was 86 inches and rain was recorded on almost two days out of every three. Rainfall in the eastern areas is much lower, about 50 inches annually. The wettest period is the late autumn and early winter. Snow falls on about twenty-five days of the year above 1,000 feet. It is usually short-lived but serious drifting can occur when high winds blow. Temperatures are in general four or five degrees Fahrenheit below those of the South Devon coast. Weather conditions can change very rapidly.

Natural History

A large area of Dartmoor consists of bogland, the two main bogs lying one between Okehampton and the Princetown–Moreton-hampstead road, the other in the region where the rivers of the south have their sources. These bogs are bleak and inhospitable not only to walkers but also to most flora and fauna. Vegetation consists mainly of mosses, lichens, purple moor grass and sedges. There are a few heathers and many wild flowers bloom. Animals rarely venture into the bogs but some birds, such as the curlew, lapwing and sandpiper, breed there.

Outside the bogs various species of heather give the Moor its characteristic appearance, the most common being *Calluna vulgaris*, the true heather. Grass, gorse and whortleberries also grow but a significant and unfortunate recent development is the wide-scale spread of bracken. This is probably partly the result of swaling, that is burning the heather to create better pasturage for domestic animals. Where the swaling is indiscriminate the heather is weakened and is replaced by bracken.

Oaks and other deciduous trees have for long graced the Moor, but conifers have been planted on open moorland and the Forestry Commission now control large plantations. Three ancient woodland copses have survived—Wistman's Wood, Black Tor Beare and Piles Copse. The oaks here are several hundred years old and the beautiful colours of their foliage create an environment quite different from any found elsewhere on the Moor. Other areas of woodland are found in some valleys such as those of the Dart and Teign.

A delightful attraction of the Moor is the ponies which are allowed to run wild but are nevertheless under private ownership. At the round-ups, or drifts, in the autumn new foals receive their owners' brands and many animals are bought and sold. The Dartmoor ponies have become so used to vehicles and their occupants that they can be a nuisance and the public are now forbidden to feed them. The ponies are probably not related to the wild horse as once thought, but more likely were turned on to the Moor in the early medieval period since when they have to some extent intercrossed with other types of horses.

Sheep and cattle are also pastured on the Moor. The main breed of sheep is the Scotch black-faced which can withstand adverse weather. The cattle are mainly the hard Galloways which are summered on the Moor and then sold for fattening. Foxes find the Moor a happy hunting ground even though the rabbit population has been decimated by myxamatosis. Badgers and otters are also common though rarely seen and the small mammals such as weasels and stoats are found in woodland areas. Bats, lizards and adders are abundant. Adders prefer rocky terrain; they are very timid and disappear as soon as they sense an intruder.

Antiquities

The antiquities of Dartmoor are remarkable for their number and diversity. They range in date from the Stone Age through the

Bronze Age to the Middle Ages and the Industrial Revolution. The survival of a large number of ancient monuments is explained partly by the lack of development of the Moor which in many respects is as it was thousands of years ago, and partly by the use of granite rather than timber for building.

The earliest remains are megalithic tombs, communal burial chambers built during the neolithic period. That at South Brent, which is covered by a cairn 130 feet long, is an outstanding example. In the Bronze Age individual tombs took the place of the communal chambers. From this period also date the Moor's stone circles and alignments or rows. There are twelve stone circles of diameters ranging from 60 to 110 feet. There are sixty alignments, some extending for more than a mile.

There is no evidence that in the neolithic period people actually lived on the Moor. But by the middle of the Bronze Age many settlements had been established in the form of pounds, villages and farmsteads, most of them in the south and west. The pounds were walled enclosures protecting a group of huts. The best known example is Grimspound which has twenty-four huts. The villages were composed of groups of huts. The farmsteads consisted of quite large huts, 20 to 30 feet in diameter, standing by square fields.

The hill-forts, such as those at Cranbrook and Prestonbury, are Celtic fortified settlements dating from the Iron Age. Ditches and ramparts added to the natural defences of the carefully chosen strong points.

We have little evidence of occupation of the Moor during the Roman period or for a considerable time after it. The Moor was used for pasturing animals but not until the mid-twelfth century did it have any importance. Then rich deposits of tin were discovered, prospectors flooded in and Dartmoor became the leading tin-producing area in Europe. Tin production fell as the surface deposits were worked out, but there was a second boom in the late fifteenth century as new techniques for sinking shafts were introduced allowing lower deposits to be worked.

There are many remains of the tin-mining days, though most are from later periods than these. The old blowing-houses are particularly interesting. Mining brought prosperity with it. Ashburton, Chagford, Plympton and Tavistock became Stannary towns to which tin was taken for testing and weighing and payment of duty to the Crown. The tower of Widcombe church is said to have been built by tin miners grateful for their prosperity.

Many farms were established during the medieval period. Examples of farmhouses may be seen at Yardworthy, Challacombe and Yeo. Recently excavations have also revealed abandoned medieval villages. The most interesting of these is between Great Tor and Hound Tor.

Access

The public are welcome to wander at will over the open countryside although they technically have no legal right to do so. All visitors are expected to follow the Country Code:

Guard against all risk of fire
Fasten all gates
Keep dogs under proper control
Keep to paths across farmland
Avoid damaging fences, hedges and walls
Leave no litter—take it home
Safeguard water supplies
Protect wildlife, wild plants and trees
Go carefully on country roads
Respect the life of the countryside

The Ministry of Defence training area in the north covers 27,000 acres but access is available at weekends and continuously from mid-July to mid-September.

The Park rangers and information assistants are responsible for helping and advising the public. Rangers and an access officer manage 500 miles of public footpaths and bridleways and also clear litter.

For further details concerning access, see page 93.

Roads

Good main roads skirt most of the Park. The A38 Exeter to Plymouth road along the southern border has been reconstructed and now has many of the characteristics of a motorway being dual carriageway throughout and bypassing the towns and villages through which the old road used to run. It provides easy access to

16

Bovey Tracey, Ashburton, Buckfastleigh, South Brent and Ivy-bridge. To the north of the Park and partly within it runs the A386 Plymouth to Okehampton road passing through Yelverton and near Lydford. On the eastern side of the Park the A382 runs from Bovey Tracey through Moretonhampstead to join the A30 which links Okehampton with Exeter and runs along the northern fringe of the Park.

Of these roads only the A386 crosses open moorland. But there are two main roads that run through the centre of Dartmoor, both with plenty of hills and bends but also with much delightful scenery to reward the careful motorist. The B3212 Exeter to Yelverton road passes through Dunsford, Moretonhampstead, Postbridge and Princetown. The shorter B3357 between Ashburton and Tavistock offers fewer contrasts but passes through the well-known beauty spot of Dartmeet.

There is also a limited network of minor roads, some of them steep and narrow but most affording splendid views and allowing access to some of the most attractive areas of the Moor. In the south-west a road runs through the china clay district from Ivy-bridge to Yelverton. A network of roads north-west of Ashburton links the pretty villages of Widecombe, Buckland in the Moor and Holne. From Bovey Tracey a road runs through to the Moretonhampstead–Two Bridges road and a continuation north-wards leads to the popular walking centre of Chagford. Roads lead from there to Drewsteignton and Castle Drogo.

Railways

Once a rail network surrounded Dartmoor and one line was even driven to Princetown. Now there remains only the main line between Exeter and Plymouth, which runs along the south-eastern fringes of the Park for much of its course with stations at Newton Abbot and Totnes.

Bus Services

Special bus services organized by the National Park authorities connect with normal scheduled services to provide an especially useful aid to the walker. They operate during the summer on Saturdays, Sundays and Bank Holidays also on Wednesdays during August. For details of these services obtain the leaflet issued by the National Park or consult Western National timetables.

Two so-called "Pony Express" services are operated by mini-buses. One runs between Bovey Tracey and Widecombe via Haytor Vale and the other between Buckfastleigh and Postbridge via Ashburton and Widecombe. The "Transmoor Link" is operated by double-decker buses and passengers can enjoy superb moorland views from the upper deck. The service runs between Plymouth and Moretonhampstead via Yelverton, Princetown, Postbridge and Warren House Inn. Other moorland bus routes are Paignton–Totnes–Buckfastleigh; Newton Abbot–Bovey Tracey–Lustleigh–Moretonhampstead; Exeter–Dunsford-Steps Bridge–Moretonhampstead.

Two services run from Plymouth every weekday during the summer. The "Dartmoor Link" operates to Burrator via Yelverton. The "Scenic Circular" follows a circular route from Plymouth to Cornwood, Shaugh Bridge, Bickleigh and back to Plymouth. Buses also run in the reverse direction. On Sundays and Bank Holidays there is a service from Plymouth to Cadover Bridge, Yelverton, Buckland Abbey and Milton Combe.

These moorland services offer connections with scheduled services such as those between Plymouth and Exeter and Plymouth and Tavistock.

Guided Walks

The National Park authorities organize a wide range of guided walks from various starting points daily during the summer and at weekends during the winter. The afternoon walks are informal and not too strenuous, lasting for three hours and covering about 5 miles. The six-hour walks starting in the morning are more taxing, covering up to 12 miles of fairly rough country. In the spring and autumn there are weekend-long walks based on local hotels. Each walk is led by one of fifty part-time approved guides who explain interesting natural and man-made features. Starting points include Chagford, Dartmeet, Lustleigh, Okehampton, Postbridge and Princetown. For full details write to the Dartmoor National Park Department, Guided Walks and Estate Office, Bovey Tracey.

The Youth and Schools Service

This service was formed to assist educational groups to gain the greatest possible benefit from visits to Dartmoor. A series of seventeen Study Packs are available, each of which contains teachers' notes, a pupils' work book and a set of maps of the area to a scale of six inches to the mile. The areas covered by these packs have been chosen for their wide range of educational experience. Together they cover almost one-fifth of the National Park. There is also an Information Pack available which contains a Resource Guide and other useful literature. The Youth and Schools Service also offers advice, fieldwork courses, a schools walk service and a talks service to schools and youth groups.

Accommodation

Accommodation of all kinds is available within the National Park, though facilities are of course much more plentiful in the centres outside its boundaries. Ask at information centres or apply to the Dartmoor Tourist Association, Leusdon Lodge, Poundsgate, Ashburton (tel. Poundsgate 304), which operates a booking service during the summer months. There are authorized sites for camping and caravans on the edge of the park. To park a caravan elsewhere you require the landowner's permission. Caravans may not be parked on common land.

Information

For a list of publications and for general information write to the Information Officer, Dartmoor National Park, Parke, Bovey Tracey. There is an information centre at Postbridge on the B3212 and mobile information centres are sited near the major entrance points to the Park at Newbridge (B3357), Steps Bridge (B3212), Postbridge and Tavistock.

Exeter

Angling.—Good fishing in Exeter and Tiverton canals, and in the rivers Exe, Creedy, Culm, and Clyst—for bream, carp, dace, gudgeon, perch, pike, rudd, roach and tench. Pike fishing is not allowed before October 1; for other fish the season is from mid-June to mid-March.

Banks.—Branches of all banks throughout the city.

Bowls.—Greens at Belmont and Heavitree pleasure grounds, Pinces Gardens and Cowick playing fields.

Cinemas.—*Odeon*, Sidwell Street; *A.B.C.*, London Inn Square.

Cricket.—At ground of *Devon County and Exeter Cricket Club*, West Avenue.

Dancing.—As advertised locally, in hotels and public halls.

Early Closing Day.—Wednesday/Saturday.

Golf.—*Exeter Golf and Country Club*, Countess Wear.

Greyhound Racing.—County Ground.

Horse Racing.—Haldon Race Club; meetings held at excellent course with 2 mile circuit, just outside city, during August and September.

Hunting.—East Devon, Mid Devon, Silverton and Tiverton hunt in the area.

Libraries.—Public Library and Records Office in Castle Street. Cathedral Library in Bishop's Palace.

Markets.—Cattle market, Marsh Barton Road. General market at Fore Street. Market Day, Friday.

Population.—98,800.

Post Office.—Bedford Street.

Squash.—*Devon and Exeter Squash Club*, Prince of Wales Road; *Exeter Golf and Country Club*, Countess Wear.

Swimming.—Public covered swimming bath with filtered and heated water. Heavitree Road.

Tennis.—Public courts at Heavitree pleasure ground (8 hard); Pinces Gardens (2 hard); Cowick Barton (3 grass).

Tourist Information Centre.—Civic Centre, Dix's Field.

Various Sports Clubs.—Archery, badminton, bowls, canoeing, fencing, rowing, swimming, tennis, table-tennis, etc.

Exeter is an ancient and fascinating city. In the days of the Romans and later under the Saxons, it was a frontier outpost whose position—shelving steeply to the river Exe—gave a natural defence against the western Celts.

Later came the Norman Castle, the Cathedral, the Guildhall and other medieval buildings, and the steady growth of the city up to our own times.

In 1942 air-raids inflicted widespread destruction. Much of great beauty and interest was lost, while the main shopping centre was

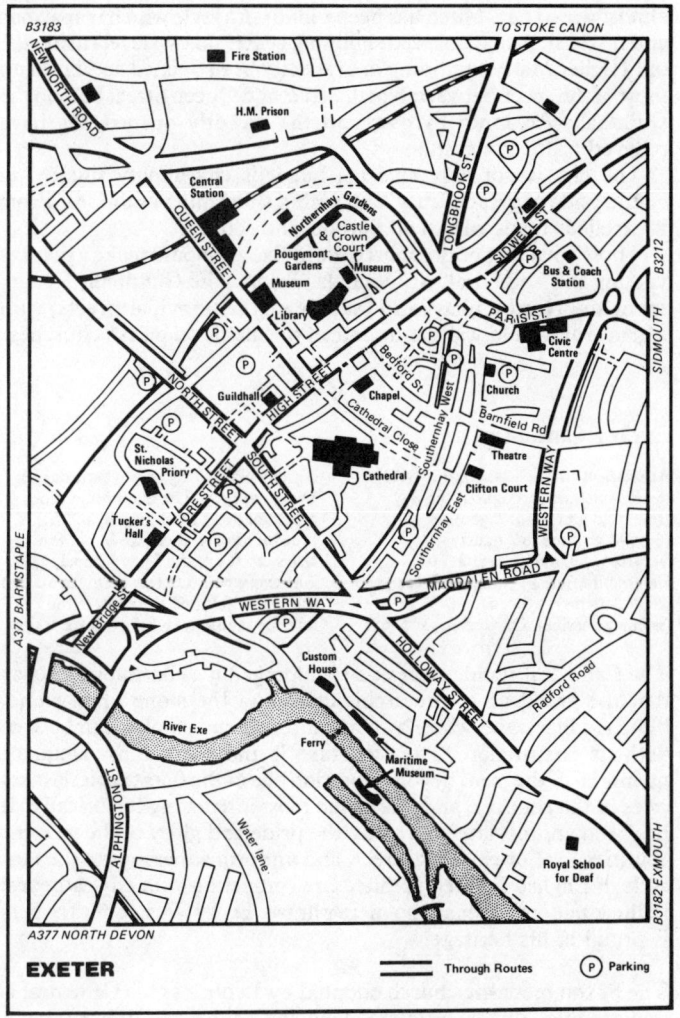

EXETER · · · · · · · Through Routes · ⓟ Parking

almost wiped out. Much has been rebuilt in a style which is spacious and modern. A new covered shopping centre on two levels using the old Higher Market building has recently been opened and takes up most of the space between North Street and Queen Street behind the Guildhall. An inner by-pass and the recently opened M5 have relieved traffic congestion.

The city is not only ancient, but it is charmingly situated in countryside of great beauty, and within a few miles of the sea. From it excellent roads run to all parts of the county.

Those spending only a short time in Exeter should make a point of visiting the Cathedral, St. Nicholas Priory, the Guildhall, Rougemont and Northernhay, and walk down the principal streets, with a glance at the old walls and some of the medieval parish churches.

Exeter Cathedral

Admission.—The Cathedral is freely open to visitors throughout the day from 7.30 a.m. until 5.30 p.m. (6.30–8.30 June to August).
Services.—On Sundays: 8 (Holy Communion), 9.45 (sung Eucharist), 11.15 (matins), 3 (evensong), 6.30 (evening service). On weekdays: 7.30 (Friday 9.30), 7.45, 5.30 (Saturday 3).
Dimensions.—The main dimensions are as follows. Total length, 408 ft.; breadth of nave choir, 40 ft.; of the aisles, 20 ft.; of the Lady Chapel, 35 ft. The transept is 140 feet long; the roof of the Cathedral is 68 feet high to the interior vaulting, and the towers, 145 ft.

The Cathedral stands clear of all buildings, in a charming close, so that the grandeur of the architecture and the stone upon stone, blotched black and white by wind and rain and smoke, can be seen without obstruction. The structure is the city's most eloquent memorial of the past, beyond question one of the finest ecclesiastical piles in the country, and one of the most interesting historically. It has been appropriately termed "the pride and glory of the western counties . . . For chaste, correct, and uniform adherence to the best style of English Pointed architecture competing with any cathedral in the kingdom". This is no mere phrase. Every West-Country man is proud of his heritage.

The Saxon monastic church adopted by Leofric as his Cathedral is said traditionally to have stood on the site of the present Lady

Chapel. Westward of this minster, William Warelwast, third Bishop of Exeter and a nephew of the Conqueror, began a newer, larger one, so that by the middle of the twelfth century a Norman Cathedral extended the whole length and width of the present nave—flanked by the great transeptal towers that have ever since been such a unique feature of Exeter—and terminated in an apse at a point where the fourth bay of the choir now ends.

The transformation of this Norman building to its present form was conceived by Bishop Bronescombe about the middle of the thirteenth century. His plan began with the erection of the Lady Chapel clear away to the eastward of the Norman apse, and on the ground where it seems likely Leofric's minister had stood; it proceeded to link this, by the present 100-feet length of Presbytery, to the Norman Choir and Nave, the whole of which was gradually rebuilt in its present lofty Gothic design.

This masterly scheme was carried on by a succession of great "Building Bishops"—Quivil, Bitton, Stapeldon, Grandisson—whose adherence to the original plan, bringing together Saxon site and Norman fabric, has given Exeter that consistently harmonious Decorated interior which is so singularly satisfying. The unusual feature of a continuous 300 ft. of graceful roof-vaulting, unbroken from west to east, is due of course to the absence of a central tower; the pair of massive flanking towers, forming transepts in their lower stages, were also fittingly altered, with higher openings and roof-arches corresponding with the rest of the building.

John de Grandisson, who ruled the diocese for over forty years and consecrated the altar in December, 1328, almost finished the edifice as it now appears, except the west front, the east window and the cloisters, which works Thomas Brantyngham (1370–94) completed. Edmund Lacy, who was translated from Hereford in 1420, and died in 1455, built the upper part of the Chapter House. The throne in the choir, the most remarkable thing of its kind in England, and the organ screen, were erected by Bishop Stapeldon (1308–26).

The Exterior

The best exterior view of the Cathedral is perhaps that which is obtained from the Cathedral yard, or **Close**. The general view of the building does not compare architecturally with that of Salisbury and

23

some other cathedrals, but only the hypercritical will deny that the pile in its old age is imposing.

The Towers. From the exterior the Norman Towers are the most noticeable features. The walls of the north tower are plain to a considerable height; it is then divided into four stages by horizontal bands, and surmounted with an embattled parapet. Each stage is adorned with arcades of round-headed arches, most of which have the zigzag moulding. Some of the arches are pierced with windows, and on the north face of this tower—and the south face of its brother—Bishop Quivil inserted a large Pointed window of six lights, with beautiful and elaborate Decorated tracery, giving light to the transepts, which are formed by the towers in their lower stages.

The towers are almost similar in general form. The south tower is the older and has more Norman arcading than the north tower: each is turned to account in quite a different way.

The North Tower contains an ancient astronomical **Clock**, traditionally supposed to have been presented by Bishop Courtenay (1478). That there was a timepiece of some sort in the Cathedral as early as Bishop Quivil's time is shown by the Patent Rolls, and by his appointing Roger of Ropeford to repair the organs and "horologe". This is the earliest record of a clock in England, but no part of it survives. In 1376–7 a new chamber was constructed in the North Transept for the "horologue called clokke". The works of an ancient instrument are in the North Transept, the "horologe" being now actuated by a modern movement (1885); the going and quarters portion, combined, are in the chamber behind (mentioned above), and the quarters strike on a small basin bell (1760) just over the dial. The disposal of parts is very much as before, the going and quarters movements being saddled one above the other. The hours are struck—as for centuries past—on the "Peter" bell in the tower above.

There are three other very early clocks in England—at Wimborne Minster, Wells Cathedral and Salisbury.

The South Tower contains thirteen of the **Cathedral Bells**. They are the second heaviest peal in England, and very rich in tone. In the North Tower hangs **Peter**, which was given to the city by Bishop Courtenay. It was recast in 1676. The Peter bell weighs 125 cwt. is

Exeter Cathedral

REFERENCE TO PLAN

A.A. Nave and Aisles.
B. St. Edmund's Chapel.
C. North Porch.
D. North or St. Paul's Tower.
E. St. Paul's Chapel.
F. South or St. John's Tower.
G. St. John the Baptist's Chapel.
H. Chapter House.
I.I. Choir and Aisles.
K. St. Andrew's Chapel.
L. St. James's Chapel.
M. St. George's Chapel.
N. St. Saviour's Chapel.
O. St. John the Evangelist's Chapel.
P. St. Gabriel's Chapel.
Q. Lady Chapel.
R. Grandisson Chapel.
T. Cloister Room, with Library over.

MONUMENTS

1. Hugh Courtenay.
3. William Sylke.
4. Bishop Lacy.
5. Bishop Stapeldon.
6. Sir John Speke, Knight.
7. Hugh Oldham.
8. Simon d'Apulia.
9. Leofric (probably).
10. Peter Quivil.
11. Bishop Bronescombe.

67 inches in diameter at the mouth, and 56 inches high, so that it ranks among the largest bells in the kingdom.

The North Porch. Close to the North Tower is the North Porch, which projects a considerable distance beyond the line of the aisles—in fact, as far out as the buttresses of the Cathedral—and is surmounted by a heavy embattled parapet. The portal has a lofty, straight, acute-angled canopy, richly crocketed. Each side is also adorned with arches and niches in which are statues presented in thank-offering for the preservation of the donor's three sons in the 1914–18 war. The largest represents St. George of England, and others St. Denis of France, St. Joseph of Belgium, St. Ambrose of Italy, St. Vladimir of Russia, St. Cyril of Serbia and St. Methodus of Roumania, the patron saints of the allied nations of the First World War. The face of the North Porch in which these figures have been placed was probably added in the fifteenth century to the main portion of it.

The West Front of the Cathedral consists of three storeys. The basement, or screen, containing the three portals, is entirely covered with niches, which are all filled with statues; above this, and receding a little, is the west wall of the nave, in which is a magnificent window, with most beautiful Decorated tracery; and above this, and receding a little in like manner behind the parapet, is the gable of the nave, containing a window of the same style, but of much smaller dimensions. The lower and greater part of the buttresses at this end of the building are hidden behind the projecting storey. The portions seen above are adorned with niches, canopies, and statues. The wall of the nave above the great west window is embattled and surmounted by hexagonal turrets, each with a canopied and crocketed pinnacle. The gable point is ornamented with a canopied niche containing a statue and teminating in a crocketed pinnacle. The screen contains three tiers (except where broken by the windows of the Grandisson Chapel) of figures of saints, kings, and other distinguished persons, somewhat damaged by the soldiers of the Parliamentary army, and also by the superstition, which lingered long in Devon, that powdered stone purloined from sacred statues possessed medicinal virtues; but much careful restoration has been carried out. On the buttresses above are two other statues—possibly

Bishop's Palace and Cathedral

Cathedral Close

King Athelstan on the north, King Edward the Confessor on the south. On the right of the centre entrance, in the space between the image-screen and the main west wall, is the tiny chapel built by Bishop Grandisson as his mortuary chapel. There are mutilated remains of a reredos on the south wall, and a figure of our Saviour sculptured on the roof. The glass (modern) of the small west window in the south aisle commemorates the Bishop; one attendant holds a model of the Cathedral, and the other that of the Church of Ottery St. Mary, which he converted into a collegiate foundation.

The Interior
The Cathedral consists of a long nave, with two aisles of the same length; north and south transepts under towers dedicated to St. Paul and St. John Baptist; and, at its eastern end, the noble Choir and aisles. The Lady Chapel, and ten other Chapels, connect with the interior at various points (*see* plan).

The Nave. The Beauty of the Nave strikes one immediately on entering. The great breadth and length, the rich windows, the uniformity of architecture, the beauty, excellence, and variety of every detail, and, above all, the form and plan of the vaulting, uninterrupted throughout the length of the Cathedral, are unrivalled in England. The roof is supported on each side upon an arcade of seven pillars and arches, the former beautifully clustered, the latter wide, but of graceful form, and wrought with mouldings and surfaces. The capitals are exquisitely moulded and of simple design; the bases, consisting of three courses of mouldings, are equally good. Between every two arches is a rich corbel, composed of figures and foliage, of which no two are alike. They support slender reeded columns of stone, with highly decorated and studiously diversified capitals, from which spring the ribs of the vaulting, which are adorned at their intersections with bosses of sculpture of various devices and exquisite finish. This roof, there being no intervening central tower or lantern, is continued across the transept to the eastern extremity of the Choir in one unbroken line, and is the longest known stone vaulting in the Pointed style of architecture.

Projecting from the north wall of the nave is the **Minstrels' Gallery**. The front is adorned with twelve niches, each containing the statue of an angel playing on a musical instrument.

A feature of the nave is the **Martyrs' Pulpit**, erected in 1877 in memory of Bishop Patteson, who suffered martyrdom in the Pacific. It is of Mansfield stone, and is an impressive specimen of modern sculpture.

From about here or perhaps a little higher up is the best view of the great **West Window**, with its magnificent fourteenth-century tracery, which formerly was filled with coloured glass in memory of Archbishop Temple (1821–1902), who was Bishop of Exeter from 1869 to 1885. The glass was all destroyed in the raid of 1942 but the new window follows the same lines.

Below to the right is a memorial tablet, in memory of Richard Doddridge Blackmore, the author of that West Country classic, *Lorna Doone*.

At the north-west angle of the nave, immediately to the left of the entrance door, is the **Chapel of St. Edmund the Martyr**, used as the chapel of the Devonshire Regiment. Divided from the nave by a beautiful parclose oak screen dating from the fourteenth century, it has been described as "nearly all window".

In the south aisle is the **Font** of Sicilian marble. It was first used in 1687.

On the south wall, a little to the west of this, hangs the Sledge Flag carried by Captain Scott on his first expedition to the Antarctic, and a little farther east a five-light window commemorates men of Devon who died in South Africa, 1899 to 1902; 467 in all. Below the window are tablets to commanders who earned fame in the same campaign—General Buller, Major-General Kekewich, defender of Kimberley.

The **Transepts** form the lowest stages of the old Norman towers, a feature shared by no other cathedral in England. **St. Paul's Chapel** (the *Children's Chapel*)—to the east of the north transept— and **St. John the Baptist's**—to the east of the south—are fitted up for private prayer and meditation. Beneath the clock in the north transept is the **Chantry Chapel of William Sylke**, a precentor of the Cathedral, his effigy, an emaciated figure in a shroud, being badly mutilated. Nearby are the old works of the clock.

The **Choir Screen** was the work of Bishop Stapeldon, who died in 1326. It is a magnificent example of the style which then prevailed, and is, as a screen, almost unrivalled in England. It is composed of three Pointed arches, richly feathered and supporting an arcade of thirteen compartments. These originally were filled with sculptured panels; they now contain paintings depicting events in Biblical history from the creation onwards; the paintings date from the seventeenth century and are more interesting than artistic. The case of the seventeenth-century organ, built by John Loosemore in 1665, remains, and contains a few of the old pipes. The present organ was erected in 1891. It is a fine sonorous instrument, recently renovated.

The Choir. In the centre of the screen is the door to the Choir. From it the very fine **East Window** may be seen to advantage. It is a nine-light Perpendicular replacement (1391) of the original window, all the other windows being Decorated, of the purest character. Nineteen whole-length figures of saints, patriarchs, and others are portrayed, six of them (three on either side in the lowest row) being survivors from the original window of *c*. 1300.

To the south of the altar are the elaborately carved sedilia of the fourteenth century, which have been admirably restored. The canopy of the seat nearest the altar, with its wreath of vine leaves, is especially beautiful. The seats themselves are possibly of an earlier date than the canopies; notice the lions which form the elbows.

Probably the most imposing feature of the Choir is the **Bishop's Throne**, of carved oak and with a pyramidal canopy of open carving rising nearly to the height of the vaulting, 52 ft. Round the base are modern paintings of Warelwast, Quivil, Stapeldon, and Grandisson—the four bishops who did most to make the Cathedral what it is.

The **Stalls** are modern, and elaborately carved with Decorated work. They, too, are of oak, the seats being formed of the old misericords, which, dating from the early part of the thirteenth century, are among the earliest existing in England. Some of them bear very curious carvings.

The **Pulpit** is modern, of oak, replacing a marble one destroyed in the air-raid of 1942.

On the north of the High Altar—the place of honour, as is his due who did so much to beautify the Choir—is the tomb of *Bishop Stapeldon* (d. 1326). The bishop was Lord High Treasurer to King Edward II and the founder of Exeter College; the effigy of a knight in armour (in the north Choir Aisle opposite) with two squires and a horse is that of his brother, Sir Richard Stapeldon: the bishop was murdered in Cheapside on account of his loyal partisanship of Edward II.

The table tomb nearby, with the indent of a lost brass on it, commemorates Bishop Lacy (d. 1455).

Beyond the Choir and Reredos is—

The Lady Chapel entered from the ambulatory aisle, or Retro-choir, at the back of the High Altar. Thought to cover the site of Leofric's Saxon monastic church, it affords a burial place for several of the Bishops of Exeter. Bishop Bronescombe began the present building, and it was finished by Bishop Peter Quivil, whose monument, a slab 9½ feet long with foliated cross and Latin inscription, is in the centre of the pavement. The Lady Chapel has a gem-like appearance, having been carefully restored and enriched with costly gifts as a memorial to the late Dean Gamble. It is 60 feet long, 35 feet wide, and 40 feet high. On the south side of the chapel are the tombs of an early Norman bishop, possibly Leofric himself, and Simon d'Apulia (1223); and on the north monuments of Sir John Doddridge, a judge of the reign of James I, and his wife, Lady Dorothy, the latter famous for the carving of the lace. On the same side the canopied tomb of Bishop Stafford (1419) separates the Lady Chapel from that of **St. John the Evangelist**, and opposite that of **St. Gabriel** is separated in like manner by the tomb and carved effigy of Bishop Bronescombe. The recumbent figure of the bishop, delicately sculptured and coloured, is considered one of the finest in existence.

At the east end of the north aisle of the Choir is **St. George's Chapel**, called also the **Chantry Chapel of Sir John Speke**, who was buried in it (1517); and in a similar position in the south aisle is **St. Saviour's Chapel**, known as **Bishop Oldham's Chantry**, that prelate having built and been interred in it (1519).

The Chapel of St. Andrew—built in the time of Bishop Bronescombe—has windows and vaulting of the same style as the north aisle of the Choir, from which it is entered. Over the chapel is the exchequer room.

St. James's Chapel, originally built at the same time as that of St. Andrew, and following the style of the south aisle, together with its ancient crypt below and the muniment room above, was destroyed during the raids of 1942 but has been rebuilt.

The Cloisters were originally built in a quadrangle south of the Cathedral, in front of the Chapter House, the north walk being designed in Bishop Orandisson's time actually under the nave buttresses. They were destroyed during the Commonwealth, and only a portion, at the south-east angle, was rebuilt in 1887. This has been glazed with stained glass preserved from the great West window when this was replaced by the Archbishop Temple memorial in 1904. The **Cloister Room** gives access to the old library above, which houses the Capitular Archives and Precentor Cook's Collection (*admission on application to new Cathedral Library*).

The **Chapter House** was built by Bishop Bruere (1224–44) in the Early English style of architecture, but the walls were heightened and the present Perpendicular windows and roof placed there nearly two centuries later. The striking frieze of figures representing the stages of the Creation was executed by local sculptor Ken Carter and installed in 1974.

The Bishop's Palace

The Bishop's Palace stands to the south-east in beautiful grounds which command the best view of the south side of the Cathedral. Here is the new **Cathedral Library**, now administered on behalf of the Dean and Chapter by the University of Exeter. The Library is open to students Monday–Friday, 2–5 p.m. It includes 20,000 books and manuscripts, among which are the "Exeter Book"; a collection of poems in Old English dating from the tenth century; the MS of "Exon. Domesday", the draft of the Domesday text for the south-western counties of England; and the original Foundation Charter of the Cathedral.

The Close

In the Close is a white marble statue by Alfred Drury of **Richard Hooker**, the celebrated divine. He was born at Heavitree in 1553.

Almost opposite the West Front of the Cathedral is the **Devon County War Memorial**, unveiled by the Prince of Wales in May, May, 1921. Designed by Sir Edwin Lutyens, a cross of Devon granite, 30 feet high, it bears the inscription: "The County of Devon. To her glorious dead, 1914–1919. Te Deum Laudamus".

In the Cathedral Yard stands the *Royal Clarence Hotel*, built about

1770, and often said to have been the first establishment in England to assume the French title of "Hotel".

When in the Close, time should certainly be spared to visit the beautiful Elizabethan building known as **Mol's Coffee House**, which is believed to have been built in 1596. The "Dutch" gable is comparatively modern. The handsome oak panelling and carving in the room on the first floor are late Elizabethan and among the forty-six coats of arms painted on the frieze are those of Drake, Raleigh, and Gilbert. The building is now used for the display of pictures, china, etc. Admission to view by courtesy. The **Annivellars' Refectory** is a few yards from Mol's Coffee House and is now part of an office suite. It was built at the beginning of the fifteenth century, the front being added in 1618. These chantry priests were called *Anivellarii* or *Annuellarii* because they celebrated the anniversaries of the deaths of their benefactors with masses. They were suppressed by Edward VI and the chantries abolished in 1549. The hall was then used for various lay purposes. The beamed roof, stone fireplace and original carved screen still remain.

Nearby is the quaint little **St. Martin's Church**, consecrated in 1065, but almost completely rebuilt in the fifteenth century of local Heavitree stone. The fine arch dividing the nave and chancel may be earlier than fifteenth century. The oak barrel-vaulted roof, the west window, font, Jacobean altar rails and west gallery are all of note. In the basement of a shop near the Royal Clarence Hotel is **St. Martin's Well** reaching a depth of 32 feet deep and connecting with underground springs.

In Catherine Street near by was the small chapel of St. Catherine founded about 1450. This was badly damaged in 1942, and only the walls remain. When the site was cleared, a Roman tessellated pavement was discovered.

Also in the Cathedral Close is the former town house of the Courtenays, now the home of the **Devon and Exeter Institution** for promoting Science, Literature, and the Arts. The hall of the adjacent building has a fine timbered Perpendicular roof with carved corbels, and a minstrels' gallery. The Jacobean oak door beyond, with its wicket gate and the arms of Bishop Cotton above, opens into a picturesque quadrangle, the residence of the Bishop of Crediton; the mullioned windows of the hall and porch, and the tracery of the windows in the chapel, together with the other details,

33

make a charming picture. The **Deanery** is the large house to the south-west of the Cathedral surrounded by a high wall and bearing the official arms of the Dean of Exeter over the entrance door. The building has a medieval hall with a fourteenth-century roof, minstrels' gallery and lancet window. It is not open to visitors. The House of the Archdeacon of Totnes is in the eastern part of the Close, the front being of Georgian design. Of the three houses which once faced this house only one survived the raids of 1942. This was formerly the residence of the Archdeacon of Barnstaple. Below the Deanery stands the **Chantry**, which is a modern replacement and now houses the Cathedral School. The Hall of the Vicars Choral in South Street was almost completely destroyed in 1942.

Old Parish Churches

The medieval parish churches of Exeter, with their red sandstone towers, have sadly decreased in numbers. They were restricted to nineteen after the Norman Conquest, and have since been reduced further by disuse, amalgamation, and man's destruction.

Though small, they are of considerable interest. Most still show signs of Norman and pre-Norman work, and are rich in mural monuments that epitomize the history of the city.

The most interesting of the churches that remain are:

St Petrock, at the centre of the parish of old Exeter. A church has existed here since the days of Athelstan.

St. Martin (*see above*) in Cathedral Yard.

St. Stephen (High Street) which was founded before the Conquest, later fell into disuse, and was rebuilt about 1664 after destruction by fire. It is now united with St. Martin.

St. Pancras (behind Guildhall), a pre-Saxon foundation on the site of the Roman Praetorium. The present church is twelfth century and possesses a fine Norman font.

St. Mary Arches (Mary Arches Street, off Fore Street) is also largely twelfth century, with Saxon work in the east wall, and a double Norman arcade. It has undergone reconstruction after severe bomb damage; the timber to restore the roof came from an American landing barge used on D-day.

St. Mary Steps (p. 39) in West Street.

St. Thomas (p. 38) is a larger church, outside the city walls and across the Exe.

St. Nicholas Priory

Another ancient ecclesiastical building that should not be missed is the Priory of St. Nicholas, in The Mint, turning out of Fore Street. Possibly the last surviving English example of a monastic guest house, the Priory has a fine eleventh-century crypt, an exceptional fifteenth-century guest hall and some sixteenth-century plasterwork. It contains some good English sixteenth-century and seventeenth-century furniture. This building, the entire western range of the original priory, is the only complete "guest house" of an ancient monastery that has survived in the whole country. *Open Tuesday to Saturday 10–1, 2–5.30.*

The Guildhall

Next to its Cathedral, Exeter glories in the ancient Guildhall. Rebuilt in 1330 and restored about a century later, it is probably the oldest municipal building in England. *Open Monday to Saturday 10–5.30 except when required for meetings.*

Formerly, it is believed, there was a Saxon building on this site. The particularly fine oak roof was erected in 1468. The beautiful Elizabethan portico which projects across the footway was added in 1593. The **Guildhall** is a handsome room with old panelling which has a frieze emblazoned with the armorial shields of ancient incorporated trades of the city and its most famous citizens. On the walls hang several portraits, not the least interesting being that by *Lely* of the Princess Henrietta Anne, daughter of King Charles I, who was born June 16, 1644, at Bedford House, which once stood on what later became Bedford Circus.

Another interesting portrait, also by Lely, is that of General Monk, afterwards Duke of Albermarle. The flags of Canada, Australia, New Zealand, and South Africa were presented to the City by the Dominions. More recent additions are the Polish and American flags, the latter presented in 1943, whilst in the gallery is the white ensign of H.M.S. *Exeter*. This was flown during the battle of the River Plate. Other portraits are hung in the **Mayor's Parlour**, above the porch, where the mantelpiece is made of lava brought from Poltimore, $3\frac{1}{2}$ miles north-east of Exeter. This room, originally a chapel, was used in the Stuart period as a prison. Later it was an assembly room for the merchant adventurers, and after that a council chamber. It contains interesting portraits, furniture and china.

On the landing outside may be seen the City regalia, which includes many beautiful specimens of the goldsmith's art, ancient and modern.

Far older than the Guildhall is—

Rougemont Castle

The Castle adjoins Northernhay, close to the Central Station, and is approached from High Street by way of Castle Street. Shakespeare tells us that the name raised the fears of Richard III when he first heard it. The Castle—or rather the small piece that remains—was built by the Conqueror, and probably received its name from the red sandstone of which it was composed. A writer of the days of Charles I called it "an old ruyning castle, whose gaping chinks and aged countenance presageth a downfall ere longe"; and the "downfall" then "presaged" was soon afterwards expedited by the unkind treatment the building received at the hands of the Roundheads under Fairfax. The ancient gateway has been restored, and beyond it is the old castle yard, in which stands a full-length *Statue of Hugh, Earl Fortescue*. Behind this statue is the **Exeter Crown Court**, in which is a large picture of "The Judgment of Daniel", painted by Brockedon, and presented by him to his native county. Round the castle yard run the ramparts, on the two outer sides forming part of the old **City Wall**, from which glimpses of the city and surrounding country can be obtained.

Close to the gateway of the castle yard is the entrance gate to Rougemont House and Gardens. The former houses the **Rouge-mont House Museum** (*Tuesday to Saturday 10–1, 2–5.30*) devoted to the history of Exeter and Devon. The **Rougemont Gardens** (*open daily to dusk*) were purchased by the council in 1913 and with their shady paths and terraced slopes make a delightful retreat. Here too is part of the castle fosse.

From the Rougemont Gardens an archway in the wall, on the level, or through **Athelstan's Tower**, if the ascending path on the right is taken, gives access to **Northernhay Gardens**, Exeter's famous promenade and open-air resort, claimed to be the first public park in England.

The City Walls. Rougemont Castle was the main defence of ancient Exeter, and perhaps the best idea of the old wall may be obtained in its vicinity, but the interested visitor may desire to see more. The original walls were probably built about A.D. 930, and are best seen in Southernhay where the surrounding buildings were destroyed in the air-raids. It is possible to make almost a circuit of the walls although the only part of the wall that can be actually promenaded is between New Bridge Street and Bartholomew Street East. Leaving Northernhay by the Queen Street entrance, the road is crossed to Northernhay Street opposite, and a little way down on the left is an arch in the wall itself, which formerly led into Maddock's Row. Close at hand is the legendary site of Athelstan's Palace. On the Iron Bridge, just above where Northernhay Street joins North Street, is a short stone pillar, with a flag-staff, erected to commemorate the Diamond Jubilee and the site of the **North Gate**, pulled down in 1769; a facsimile of the gate is shown with the original weather vane. It is unfortunate that none of the medieval gates remain, but plaques mark their sites. Beyond Iron Bridge, on the city side, is Bartholomew Street, and here one follows the wall itself, the typical rampart of a walled city, with widespreading views across the river to the hills beyond. The **East Gate** stood at the end of High Street, near the modern cinema. Near St. Mary Steps Church in West Street is the space where the **West Gate** stood, as recorded on a tablet. Crossing the inner by-pass and continuing along Lower Coombe Street, one is almost on the wall again, and keeping down Quay Hill and turning sharp to the right under it, what remains of the Water Gate may be seen. By taking Quay Lane on the left South Street is reached, but there is nothing but a bronze tablet to show where the **South Gate** stood close to Trinity Church. Two sections of the old wall in Quay Lane collapsed in 1927; the remaining parts, cemented and made secure, show a difference in level of some 20 feet between the city wall within the wall and the outside.

Principal Streets

High Street is the chief street of the city, and under the names of New Bridge Street, Fore Street, High Street and Sidwell Street, it extends from the Exe Bridge to the north-eastern suburbs. The antiquary Leland declared that "there be diverse fair Streates in Excester, but the High Streate, that goith from the West to the Est Gate, is the fairest". It may have been the main Roman road and is certainly the most important and probably the oldest street in

Exeter. The air-raids of 1942 destroyed many of its ancient buildings as well as more modern developments, but some old buildings
remain. The Red Brick House opposite Queen Street is of
seventeenth-century Dutch architecture, made from bricks brought
from Holland. Other old houses, apart from those in the Cathedral
Close and High Street, can be seen at Stepcote Hill; and the Tudor
House stands in West Street.

The old waterfront is worth a visit. The Quay with its enormous
nineteenth-century warehouses, has been the setting for the tele-
vision series "The Onedin Line" on many occasions. The **Custom
House**, dated 1681, contains fine plasterwork ceilings and a Charles
II coat of arms. Visitors may view the interior by arrangement with
HM Customs and Excise.

On the Quay and beside the Basin the **Maritime Museum** (*daily,
summer 10–6, winter 10–5*) has the largest boat collection of its kind
in the world. Nearly one hundred craft are on display, either afloat
or under cover. Exhibits include the world's oldest working steam-
boat and boats that have been rowed across the Atlantic and Pacific
Oceans.

The centre of Roman Exeter, where North Street and South
Street join High Street, was formerly known as the **Carfax** (Lat.
quadrifurcus) or cross-roads. The western extension of High Street
originally bore left at the Guildhall and ran down Stepcote Hill to the
river Exe.

A short distance down Fore Street on the right is the **Tucker's
Hall**, or the Hall of "The Worshipful Company of Weavers, Fullers
and Shearmen", to give it its full title (*shown Tuesdays, Thursdays
and Fridays 10.30 to 12.30 in summer: Fridays 10.30 to 12.30 in
winter*). Built in 1471–2 as the "Lady Chapel of the Tuckers and
Weavers", it was divided by a substantial floor into lower and upper
halls about 1634; the fine roof and panelled walls are still displayed
upstairs.

Fore Street and New Bridge Street continue downhill to **Exe
Bridge**, across which is the **Church of St. Thomas**, whose vicar in
1549 was hanged on the tower as a rebel.

In the neighbourhood of the bridges, on the east side of the river,
there is much that is noteworthy for those interested in church and
domestic architecture. In Tudor Street, behind the new block of
office buildings stands an Elizabethan merchant's house.

In West Street is the parish church of **St. Mary Steps**, founded in the twelfth century. The richly ornamented tub font is of this period. The present fabric dates largely from the fifteenth century, when the church was enlarged. Of the screen only three bays, enclosing the south aisle chapel, belong to that century, and even these were not original to the church, but were taken from the medieval church of St. Mary Major when it was demolished in the middle of the last century; the other five bays across the chancel were constructed at that time by Harry Hems. The fine east window of Christ in majesty, by John Hayward, was introduced in 1697. Over the high altar is a tester bearing the Tetragrammaton—the Hebrew letters of the name Jehovah or YHWH. Outside the south face of the tower are clock jacks which strike the hour and quarters. The clock and the central figure date from the early seventeenth century; the other figures are considerably later.

Close by the church some fifteenth-century merchants' houses have been preserved and restored. Two stand at the foot of **Stepcote Hill**, which in medieval times was the main street into the city from the west. The third, thought to be one of the oldest timber-framed houses in Europe, was removed bodily in 1961 from its site in Edmund Street three hundred feet up the slope to its present position on the corner of West Street. Adjacent to this house are the remains of the **West Gate**, and part of the west wall of the city. Further parts of the wall may be seen on the river side of the inner by-pass. Between the site of the West Gate and the river can be seen the exposed arches of the first stone bridge across the Exe, with the ruined **Church of St. Edmund** standing beside it.

Turning up Coombe Street into South Street and continuing into Magdalen Street, we reach the Eye Infirmary. Opposite are the picturesque red stone former almshouses known as **Wynard's Hospital**. An archway leads into the cobble-stoned courtyard round three sides of which the dormer-windowed houses of twelve pensioners were built, the chapel and the widows' quarters occupying the fourth side. They were built in 1430 by William Wynard, a Recorder of Exeter, but were converted in 1972 into offices for various voluntary bodies.

Exeter was, and to some extent still is, rich in almshouses. A little nearer Southernhay a stone in the wall on the same side marks the former site of Palmer's Almshouses for four poor women, endowed in 1487, and some distance beyond Wynard's are the rebuilt **Magdalen Almshouses**, the old leper hospital. Still farther, at the junction with Heavitree Road, is **Livery Dole**, with its ancient chapel and newer dwellings, begun by Sir Robert Dennis in 1591. If this does not satisfy interest in such foundations, a journey may be made to the top of Sidwell Street, in which, at the beginning of Old Tiverton Road, are **St. Anne's Almshouses**. St. Anne's Day, July 26, has been observed here for centuries.

At the junction of Denmark Road and Barnfield roads is the **Martyrs' Memorial**, commemorating the Martyrdom of Thomas Benet, M.A., burnt at Livery Dole in 1531, and Agnes Prest, who suffered the same fate on Southernhay in August, 1557, the then mayor refusing to allow the execution within the city wall.

By keeping to the left, High Street can be regained *via* Barnfield Road. Bedford Circus, containing the earliest houses of Georgian Exeter, was entirely destroyed by bombing. Much attractive Georgian architecture can, however, still be seen in Barnfield Crescent, in Southernhay West, and in other parts of the City outside the walls. Retracing one's steps down High Street into **Queen Street**, a visit can be paid to the—

Royal Albert Memorial Museum and Art Gallery

A Gothic building, erected in 1865–9 as a memorial to the Prince Consort. It houses one of the largest collections in the region with fine paintings and watercolours, collections of costumes, silver and glass, and sections on ethnography, foreign archaeology and natural history. *Open Tuesday and Saturday, 10–5.30.*

The Underground Passages

A unique feature in Exeter is the complex of medieval underground water courses from which the growing population of the Cathedral complex and the City were supplied with wholesome water from the Well of St. Sidwella outside the City Walls between Longbrook Street and Sidwell Street. *Tuesday to Saturday 2–5.*

The **City Library** is in Castle Street. The former library was burnt out in the war and the new building was opened in 1965. The West Country Studies Library occupies part of it. This contains a wealth of printed material about the area. The search rooms of the City Record Office adjoin the Library.

The **University of Exeter** caters for 4,500 students on the

270-acre campus to the north of Exeter. The Extra-Mural Department is still in the old Gandy Street building. The Department of Education occupies the former St. Lukes College building in Heavitree Road.

Countess Wear

Three miles down river from Exeter is Countess Wear, set amid delightful surroundings which, time and again, have inspired the painter's brush. The old bridge has yielded to the demands of modern traffic and now forms an important road link although the bridge has been scheduled as an ancient monument. A good way to the Wear is to take the ferry at Topsham and walk up the Canal towpath (west bank).

It is stated that the River Exe once flowed deep with the tide as high as Exeter, but in 1282 it was closed to salt water and sea-going vessels by the erection of a weir, the work of the then Countess of Devon, who thus revenged herself upon the citizens for some affront. Thus arose the name "Countess Wear". An opening was made in the obstruction, but some years later the Earl of Devon "maliciously destroyed the haven" in revenge for a dispute concerning the distribution of some fish. The Exeter people, to re-establish communication with the sea, constructed a canal from the City to a point just below Countess Wear, which was opened early in Elizabeth's reign; since then it has been twice extended, its present terminus being Turf.

Topsham

About five miles down river from Exeter is Topsham, formerly an important sea-port and now incorporated in the city. Topsham has a long and honourable past. Part of it lies on one of the roads to Exmouth, but the part that does not remains a quiet and peaceful village bordering the River Exe. Its streets contain many delightful examples of domestic architecture.

The **Church** is modern except for its red sandstone tower, and is notable for its fine position overlooking the Exe, and for two monuments by Chantry—to Admiral Sir John Duckworth and to his son. In the Strand (No. 25) there is a small museum devoted to the history of this ancient River Exe port. From Topsham the eastern bank of the Exe can be followed to Exmouth.

Excursions from Exeter

1. To Crediton and Chulmleigh

Leave Exeter by the A377 Barnstaple road which leads in 8 miles to—

Crediton

This busy country town of about 5,700 people is recorded as the birthplace of St. Boniface in about 680 and a minster was established in 739. But Crediton is likely to disappoint those who expect to find an ancient town. It is almost entirely modern, having suffered from several fires. "As fine as Kirton spinning" has lost its significance since cloth-making is no longer carried out having been superseded by a number of light industries.

Many of the buildings are of local sandstone including the majestic **Church**. Most of the present building is Perpendicular but the base of the tower is Transitional Norman. The large clerestory windows are a notable feature, and the east and west windows are also fine, but during restoration the former, distinctive if not unique, was spoilt by being altered to conform with the other. The choir aisles lead through arches into the Lady Chapel, originally Early English in style, which served as the Grammar School from 1572 until 1860. In the south choir aisle is a fourteenth-century altar tomb, supposed to be that of Sir John Sully and his wife; he lived to a great age, fought at Crécy and Poictiers and in other battles. Near the Altar is the monument of Sir William Periam, an Elizabethan Chief Baron of the Exchequer, reclining in his robes, and next is one of the seventeenth century to members of the Tuckfield family. Over the tower arch at the east end of the nave is a memorial to General Buller. The mutilated stone sedilia, with what may be a tomb behind them, and the Norman font are worth noting. In the north aisle is a richly carved chest, *c.* 1420 in date, depicting on its panels *The Adoration of the Shepherds*. When the bishopric was removed to Exeter the church was made collegiate and it remained so until the Dissolution. Edward VI sold it to twelve citizens for £200 and their successors are still called the Twelve Governors.

Near St. Lawrence Green at the top of the town, formerly the scene of fairs and bull-baiting, just off the main road is **Lawrence Chapel**, once a chantry but now used as a school chapel. Off the Tiverton road, in the cemetery, is the ancient **Chapel of St. John the Baptist**, re-erected in 1925 after removal from an isolated site near Thorverton. Records show the building was in existence in 1425.

About 8 miles beyond Crediton a right turn leads to **Lapford**. The fifteenth-century church is outstanding for its beautifully carved screen and Tudor bench-ends.

Continue along the A377 for 5 miles when another right turn leads to **Chulmleigh** attractively set in the valley of the Little Dart. The church contains a magnificent rood-screen retaining some of its original colouring and stretching more than 50 feet across the nave and aisles. The wagon roof is adorned with angels and variously carved bosses.

2. To Okehampton

Leave Exeter by the A30 Okehampton road and in 12 miles shortly after bypassing Crockernwell take a left turn to reach—

Drewsteignton

The attractive village displays a pleasing combination of Dartmoor granite and the softer whitewashed Devon cottages. It is situated on the eastern fringes of Dartmoor in beautiful countryside. To the east are the remains of the Iron Age fort of **Prestonbury Castle** overlooking the well-known beauty spot **Fingle Bridge**. The granite bridge dating from the sixteenth century spans the romantic Fingle Gorge. But the main attraction is **Castle Drogo** (*Easter to October, daily 11–6*), which stands 900 feet above the gorge of the River Teign enjoying wonderful views on all sides. This granite castle, the last great house to be built in England, was built between 1910 and 1930 by Sir Edwin Lutyens and has been in the possession of the National Trust since 1975. See also page 98.

For Chagford to the south-west, see page 64.

The main road continues along the northern border of the

National Park to **Sticklepath**. This is the home of **Finch's Foundry**, a nineteenth-century tool works restored to working order. Three water wheels are the most spectacular of the many pieces of equipment that may be seen in operation on certain days. The foundry also houses the **Sticklepath Museum of Rural Industry** (*daily 11–6*).

The pretty village of **Belstone**, a mile to the south-west, retains its stocks and there is an interesting ancient stone in the churchyard. The **Nine Maidens** on nearby Belstone Tor were, the story goes, nine girls who were turned to stone for dancing on the Sabbath.

The main road shortly reaches—

Okehampton

Distances.—Barnstaple, 36 miles; Bodmin, 41; Bude, 29; Exeter, 23; London, 197; Plymouth, 31.
Early Closing Day.—Wednesday.
Fishing.—Trout fishing in East and West Ockment rivers.

Golf.—18-hole course in Okehampton Park.
Library.—Fore Street.
Population.—4,000.
Tennis.—Simmons Park.

Okehampton is situated between the East and West Ockment rivers which unite just below the town. Lying just outside the National Park at its north-western corner, it is an excellent centre for tours and trips in beautiful scenery. It is also an important commercial centre for the area and its shopping facilities include a modern pedestrian precinct. A by-pass is planned to relieve the heavy traffic experienced during the summer.

Substantial remains of the large **Castle** (*March and October, weekdays 9.30–5.30, Sunday 2–5.30; April, daily 9.30–5.30; May to September, daily 9.30–7; November to February, weekdays 9.30–4, Sunday 2–4*) stand on the summit of a rock near the Launceston road close to the left bank of the West Ockment, about ½ mile south-west of the town. The site commands a wide view of the valley. The ruins, which date mainly from the fourteenth century, include a small rectangular keep, part of the outer gate near the river, portions of the great hall with its huge chimney and old baking ovens at the back, and the chapel.

For a walk or ride in the Okehampton area, see page 117.

Fingle Bridge

3. To Moretonhampstead and Princetown

Dartmoor is almost bisected by the B3212 running across it from north-east to south-west and forming a more attractive though more arduous route to Plymouth than the A30 main road through Ashburton and Ivybridge. Leaving Exeter by way of Pocombe Bridge and Longdown, the road begins to traverse the Moor not far beyond Moretonhampstead.

About 7 miles from Exeter take a left turn along the B3193 and in 2 miles turn left again to **Doddiscombsleigh** where the church is famous for its medieval stained glass. It fills five windows in the north aisle, the finest perhaps being the most easterly depicting the seven sacraments. To the south lies the village of **Higher Ashton** whose church has a richly carved fifteenth-century screen with a number of painted panels.

Return to the main road from which almost at once a right turn leads to **Dunsford**, a pretty village with thatched cottages above the

Overleaf North Bovey

Teign. The church contains a magnificent seventeenth-century monument to Sir Thomas Fulford who lies with his wife and seven children. The main road continues through attractive scenery, crossing the Teign at **Steps Bridge** which is the starting-point of a nature trail.

About 13 miles after leaving Exeter we reach **Moretonhampstead**, a favourite centre for Dartmoor. A former market town of some importance, it is prettily situated on sloping ground. The impressive Perpendicular church of granite has a fine tower. Also of interest are the former almshouses built of granite in 1637 with a stone colonnade. For a walk in the area see page 105.

From the town a southward turning leads to the peaceful and pretty old-world village of **North Bovey**, a place well worth a visit. The unpretentious village cross at one time served as a footbridge across the Bovey, but is now restored to a more dignified position. In the church are carved roof bosses representing Edward I and his queens. The oak pulpit, chancel screen and bench ends also display interesting carvings. See also page 106.

In about 2 miles we reach a cross-roads at which the right turn leads to Chagford (see page 64) and on the left the B3344 should be taken for Widecombe-in-the-Moor (see page 74). We continue along the B3212 for a further mile where a road strikes southwards to—

Grimspound

Here massive granite blocks form an irregular wall, some 150 yards long by 120 broad, around an area of about four acres. The height of the wall now is only some 3 or 4 feet, but there are indications that this was probably more than double originally, and that the walls were in addition surmounted by a sort of turf parapet. There are entrances south, east and west, the former, paved, being the oldest, and a pathway or track passes through, leading from Manaton to Headland Warren. The ruins of some twenty-four hut-circles within the enclosure, one of which has been restored, and most of which were undoubtedly at one time inhabited, prove the existence here of a prehistoric village, probably of the Early Bronze period. The wall kept wild animals out and ensured a place of safety for flocks and herds. See also page 110.

The main road continues past *Warren House Inn* south-westward to—

Postbridge

The village is famous for one of the most perfect existing specimens of the old clapper bridges. It consists of four granite piers supporting four great granite slabs, one at each end and two side by side in the centre. The bridge stands some seven feet above the river and is 42 feet 8 inches long. The old clapper at Postbridge has withstood the fury of the East Dart for centuries, and may still be used without the slightest risk. The ancient paved trackway, which is distinct from the pack-horse road, can be traced for some distance to the west of the Dart, and there are many interesting remains in the neighbourhood. For a walk in the area, see page 118.

Just before reaching **Two Bridges**, where we cross the highway connecting Ashburton and Tavistock, the Princetown road passes on the right **Crockern Tor** (1,391 ft.), sometimes called the Parliament Rock. There is a venerable authority for the statement that from the reign of Edward I until the middle of the eighteenth century the Stannary Court—the parliament of the tinners—was held here. Tavistock, Plympton, Ashburton and Chagford each sent to it twenty-four burgesses, whose duty it was to enact laws and regulations, which, when ratified by the Lord Warden of the Stannaries, were binding. The privileges accorded to the tinners, and the arbitrary character of many of their acts, are proverbial in Devon and Cornwall. In later times, it became the custom of the court to meet here and go through the preliminary forms; and then, owing to the bleak and exposed situation, to adjourn for the transaction of business to one of the Stannary towns, generally Tavistock.

Wistman's Wood, a little to the north of Crockern Tor, is equally interesting. It occupies the side of a hill overlooking the *West Dart*, and covers an area about 700 yards long by a hundred wide. The wood consists of a few clumps of stunted oaks, which have existed for centuries with but little change. Though ivy and other parasitic plants entwine them there is encouraging evidence of regeneration.

A mile beyond Two Bridges lies—

Princetown

This favourite stopping place for coach trippers is so called in honour of the Prince of Wales, afterwards George IV, because it and much of Dartmoor form part of the estates of the Duchy of Cornwall. It owes its origin to the persistent efforts of an eighteenth-century worthy who imagined that a fortune was to be won by the exploitation of Dartmoor. This gentleman, Sir Thomas Tyrwhitt, was secretary to the Council of the Prince of Wales, and Member of Parliament successively for Okehampton and Plymouth. It was at his suggestion that the locality was selected in 1806 as the site of a prison for the army of Frenchmen who had been captured in the wars. Later it was used for Americans taken during the war of 1812–14. A stained-glass east window in memory of American prisoners who died was presented to the church in 1910 by the National Society of United States Daughters of 1812. The church was built by French and American prisoners, and is not far from the prison.

The high boundary wall of the present establishment encloses an area of nearly thirty acres and surrounds the buildings in which the prisoners of war were lodged, the inscription over the gateway, *Parcere subjectis* ("spare the vanquished"), being more appropriate to the prison's original purpose than to its later use. By the time the prison was built and occupied Princetown had grown into a hamlet of considerable size. When a few years later peace was proclaimed, the place fell into decay. In spite of the efforts of Tyrwhitt, it remained a deserted village until 1850, when, probably at the suggestion of the Prince Consort, who had visited it a few years before, the old war prison was used for convicts.

From the front there is little to be seen of the Prison. By far the best viewpoint is a spot on the Two Bridges road just beyond the Princetown 30 mile speed limit sign.

For walks and rides in the area, see page 120. For the continuation of the road south-westward to Yelverton and Plymouth, see page 88.

4. To Powderham and Dawlish

The A379 follows fairly closely the western bank of the River Exe. It runs through pretty country traversed by good roads, well watered and wooded, and dotted with charming villages many of which have associations with great names in English history. With the river estuary close by, the beginning of the Haldon ridge on the right, and the first of the red cliffs by Lympstone or by Dawlish rising ahead, this route forms an admirable approach to the South Devon seaboard.

About 5 miles after leaving Exeter we arrive at—

Exminster

Exminster lies on the western side of the Exe connected with Topsham by ferry. It is a large village whose history goes back to Saxon times. The fourteenth-century church was thoroughly "restored" in Victorian times, but it retains some interesting features, including the attractive tower, the ceiling of the Lady Chapel (1633) and some fine memorials. There are some interesting old houses in the neighbourhood. *Peamore* and *Matford* were originally Domesday manors. *Kenbury House* has a long history but the present building is mainly Georgian.

From Exminster it is an easy drive of 5 miles to Kenton (bus service) or Powderham.

Powderham Castle

Open April to Spring Holiday, Sunday and Bank Holidays, then daily except Friday and Saturday until mid-September. Bus stop at gates.

The beautiful country seat of the Earls of Devon is ½ mile beyond Kenton. The Castle was built about the end of the fourteenth century by Sir Philip Courtenay, younger son of Sir Hugh Courtenay, and Margaret, daughter of Humphry de Bohun, his wife. The manor of Powderham was left by will to Sir Philip by his mother, who had it as a marriage portion from her father. Only four towers and the chapel of the old structure remain, the rest of the Castle having been built at various later periods.

The park, in which many deer roam, is of great extent, and is only separated from the river by the railway, which runs along the eastern side. It is thickly planted with oaks, and on its highest ground is a tower, called the **Belvedere**, erected in 1773. The **Church** is entirely a fifteenth-century building with arcades of Beer stone; it contains an oak screen, reredos, and altar, besides several interesting memorials.

A little south-west of Powderham is the village of—

Kenton

Leland described the Church here as "a right goodly church". Built in the reign of Edward III, it is of Perpendicular architecture, with pinnacled buttresses to the south aisle, niched south porch, and tall red sandstone tower. The magnificent rood-screen believed to date from 1455 extending right across the east end of the church, is panelled and ornamented with carvings, and paintings of apostles, saints and prophets, on which are sentences from the Creed. The pulpit is coeval with the screen and at one time was broken up and destroyed, but it was possible to collect the fragments and restore it, the niches being filled with modern paintings. The capitals of the pillars merit attention and so does the south porch with its embattlements and parvise chamber.

From Kenton it is a pleasant walk over the hill north-west of the church and up the valley to **Kenn**, where the church is almost equally noteworthy. From here it is only a short distance to the main road which continues to **Starcross** which, though little more than a village, is thronged with visitors during the season. A ferry crosses the Exe to Exmouth. The most prominent object in Starcross is a massive, red sandstone building with an equally massive tower. The part surmounted by the latter was once used as a Methodist chapel, while the remainder served as stores. Originally it was one of Brunel's pumping stations in the early "atmospheric" days of the railway.

From Starcross the route may be continued by the main road or a detour made via Cockwood and Dawlish Warren, to—

Dawlish

Bathing.—Excellent from Main Beach and Coryton Cove.
Bowls.—Greens on the Lawn and at the Recreation Grounds, Exeter Road.
Buses.—To Exeter, Teignmouth, Newton Abbot and Torquay.
Early Closing.—Thursday.
Entertainments.—Band on the Lawn; Shaftesbury Theatre.

Golf.—*Warren Golf Club* on the Warren, north of the town.
Information Bureau.—The Strand.
Library.—Old Town Street.
Population.—10,000.
Tennis.—Recreation Grounds, Exeter Road.

Dawlish and Teignmouth are neighbouring resorts on the coast between the mouth of the Exe and the sandy Teign estuary, and are only three and a half miles apart. Though so close, they bear little resemblance. Dawlish is essentially pretty and *petite*—a gem among seaside resorts; the view obtained from the railway line of the Lawn with houses on either side of its green expanse, and divided down its centre by the docile Dawlish Water, suggests a dolls'-house scene. The stream flows on its way to the sea without any vulgar gurgling or

52

broiling, its water dotted with proud swans and spanned at intervals by lightly-made bridges.

There is no prettier place in its own particular style on the South Devon coast. North and south, towering red cliffs sentinel the town, and between them for a mile and a half stretches the parade, provided with seats, and pleasant in almost any weather and at any season, for Dawlish claims an equable climate.

The Lawn. A feature of Dawlish is the neatly kept Lawn, with its trim gardens, between the Strand and the "Brook"—as the Dawlish Water is locally called. On the Lawn there is a bowling green which is the scene of first-class tournaments. Among the water birds on the brook may be seen black swans—rare in this country—the progeny of parents imported from Australia.

Proceeding inland from the Lawn one comes to **Manor Grounds.** This site, in the centre of the old town, is now a public park, and the Manor House (c. 1800) occupied by local government offices. Nearby is the ancient **Parish Church of St. Gregory,** whose first recorded vicar was Capelanus in 1272. It is charmingly situated at the back of the town, about ten minutes' walk from the station. The tower and pillars are all that remain of an older foundation.

The Beach extends northward from the Marine Parade for 1½ miles to Langstone Cliffs. The sands are extensive and firm, and they slope so gradually that bathing may be enjoyed without risk.

At the southern end of the beach is **Boat Cove,** where rowing-, sailing- and motor-boats can be hired. If one follows the sea-wall southwards, past the detached red standstone rock, and mounts the zigzag path, one reaches the seats and shelters of **Lea Mount** (a breezy but shady pleasure ground presented to the town by Sir Thomas Lea). From here fine views can be obtained of the coastline, extending beyond Exmouth and Straight Point to Beer Head, and on occasion as far as Portland.

The sea wall has been continued beyond Lea Mount to **Coryton Cove,** a sheltered beach much favoured by bathers and sun-bathers. Beyond this is **Shell Cove,** popular for picnics; this cove is usually reached by boat, being accessible by land only at the lowest tide. Still farther southwards is the curious rock formation known as the **Parson and Clerk,** the subject of local legend.

Northwards from Lea Mount, the best route to Langstone Cliffs is to follow the sea-wall, except at high tide, when it may be

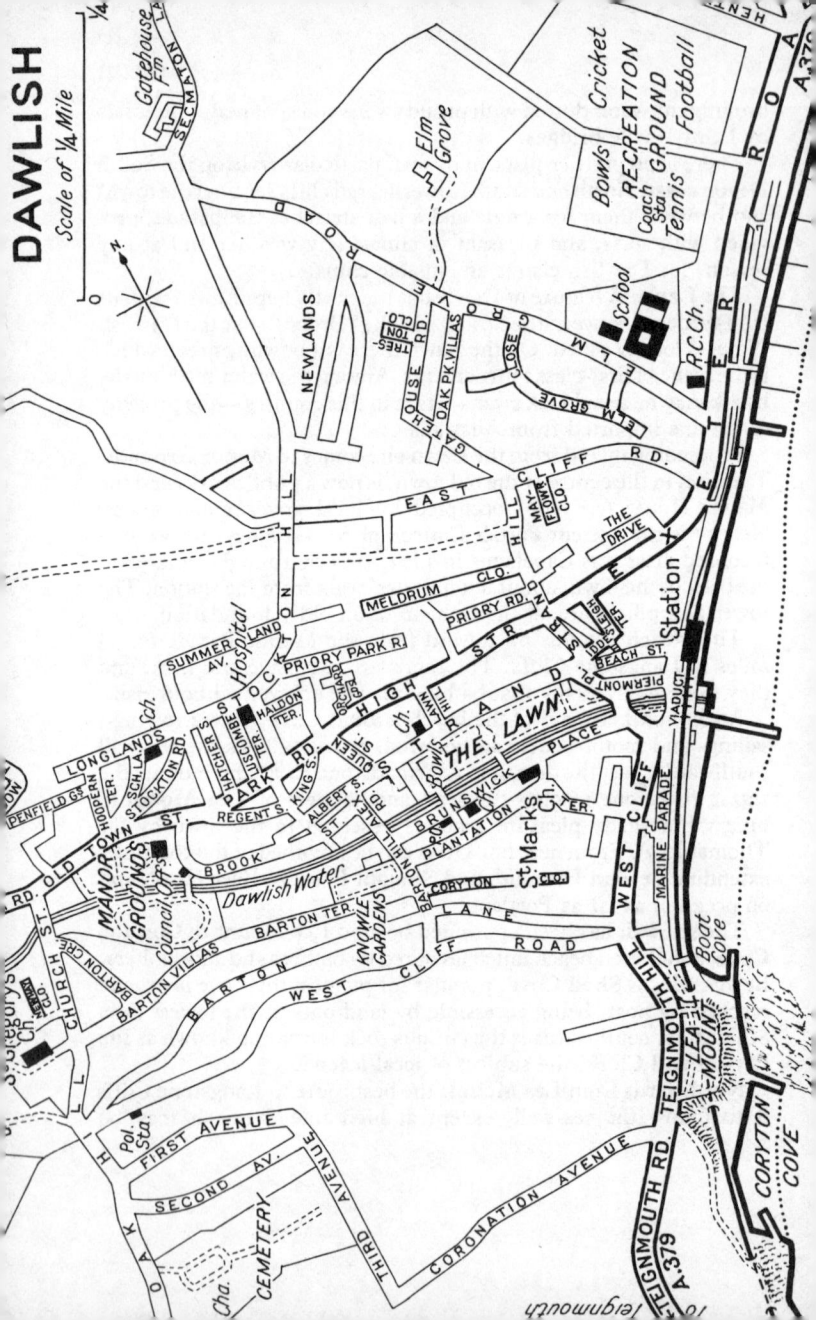

necessary to follow the Exeter Road until the footpath to **Ladies' Mile** is reached. Langstone Cliffs contain several little caves that can be explored at low water. Above the beach is **Mount Pleasant,** a wooded height on which is an hotel. An arch in the sea-face of the rocks, and a curiously shaped rock known as the **Elephant** are among the other natural attractions of the spot.

Beyond Langstone is—

The Warren, a low, sandy bar almost blocking the mouth of the Exe. It is a breezy walk across the Warren to the end of it facing Exmouth, but full of interest, for Dawlish Warren is noted for its wild bird life and for certain rare flowers. The Warren is a playground for young and old alike for it is an area which caters for most tastes. Facilities include a large car park with a capacity of 2,000 cars. A mile and a half-long stretch of fine, sandy beach, washed by the tide, offers safe bathing, boating and relaxation. Near at hand is an amusement centre, children's railway, putting and obstacle golf and also an 18-hole golf course. Beach huts are available for renting. Immediately inland from the Warren are numerous well-laid-out caravan and chalet parks and a holiday camp offering facilities for those preferring a self-catering holiday. There is also an interesting railway museum with model railway.

Newton Abbot

Access.—Newton Abbot is a major railway junction and is on the direct route from Paddington to the Torquay area, and from Liverpool and Manchester. Excellent bus services serve all parts of the area. The local bus station for the "Devon General" services is near the market. Long-distance coaches stop outside the railway station.

Bowls.—Public green in Courtenay Park.

Cinemas.—*Alexandra* and *Odeon*.

Cricket.—South Devon Cricket Club. Saturday matches in Marsh Road. Special holiday subscriptions per match for visitors.

Early Closing Day.—Thursday.

Fishing.—Salmon and trout; *Teign* and *Dart:* also coarse fishing in the five ponds of Rackerhayes and in Stover Park Lane.

Golf.—Stover Golf Club (18 holes) is 2½ miles from the town on the Bovey Tracey Road. There is a putting green at Forde Park.

Information Bureau.—Sherborne Road.

Library.—At junction of Bank, Highweek and Market Streets.

Market Day.—Cattle and Pannier, Wednesday; Pannier, Saturday.

Population.—19,940

Racing.—Under National Hunt rules. Meetings from April to September, and on Boxing Day.

Railway.—Newton Abbot station, Western Region line. Newton Abbot is a Motorail terminal.

Sailing and Canoeing.—Decoy Lake.

Swimming.—Up-to-date open-air, heated, bathing pool with diving boards, etc., at Penn Inn Park.

Tennis.—Hard courts at Baker's Park and Forde Park.

Newton Abbot is a thriving market town, and the busy centre of a large agricultural area. The town stands in a beautiful vale, watered by the River Lemon, which flows into the Teign, a short distance below the spot where that river changes its character as a boisterous moorland stream for that of a placid estuary. The little River Lemon forms the boundary between two parishes; but within the limits of the town it is mostly arched over, and the continuity of the streets and houses is unbroken.

The sports enthusiast is well catered for at Newton Abbot. There is a good cricket ground in Marsh Road belonging to the South Devon C.C., where are also tennis courts; there are public hard

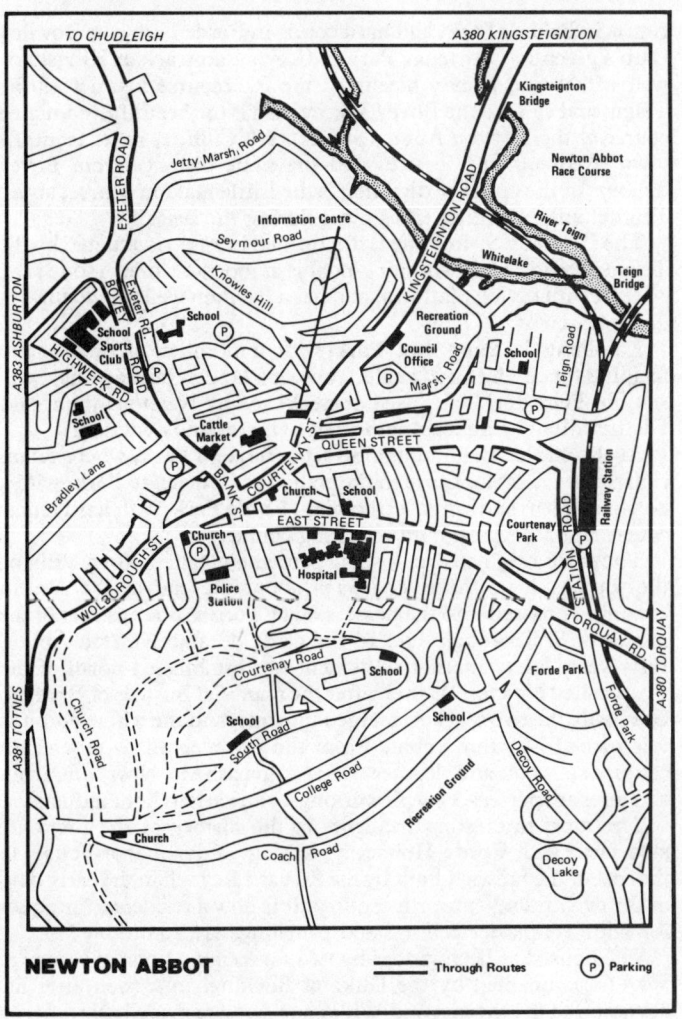

NEWTON ABBOT

Through Routes

Ⓟ Parking

courts in Baker's Park, and hard courts in Forde Park, the Bowling Club's green in Courtenay Park, a Greyhound track at Kingskerswell with twice weekly meetings, the Racecourse just across the Teign, and close to the Bovey Tracey road is the beautifully situated course of the Newton Abbot (Stover) Golf Club, 2½ miles from the town (frequent bus service) and the same distance from Bovey Tracey. In the opposite direction is the Little Haldon course, above Teignmouth. Hunting takes place during the season.

The **Penn Inn Swimming Bath,** opened in 1935, is situated by the Torquay road. The swimming-pool is an open-air one, 120 feet by 40 feet, with diving platform, and has a Pavilion well provided with dressing-rooms.

Adjoining is **Penn Inn Park** with a number of amusement facilities for children and a café. There is a Model Railway track with station, Penn Inn Halt, used at weekends by Newton Abbot and District Model Engineering Society. Operation is voluntary.

At the end of Wolborough Street is **Baker's Park,** where tennis courts are available. Close to the station is **Courtenay Park,** with a bowling green, and, almost adjoining, **Forde Park,** with hard tennis courts and a pavilion, and a putting course.

The town originated in a small settlement called **Nova Villa** on the south side of the river *Lemon* about the end of the twelfth century. It passed into the possession of Torre Abbey as part of the manor of Wolborough, and so the name became Newton Abbot. Fifty years later, another settlement was established north of the river, called **Newton Bushel,** after the manorial Bushels of Bradley. Gradually the two markets merged into one, and the whole borough was named Newton Abbot. From the seventeenth to nineteenth centuries, wool and leather trades flourished. Now the main activities are pottery, clay pit workings, and various light industries.

The most interesting incidents in the history of the town are associated with **Forde House,** a pleasing Tudor manor-house, to the east of the railway, built by Sir Richard Reynell in the early days of the eventful seventeenth century. It is now a residence (antiques for sale). Its plaster ceilings and panellings are admirable.

The house has been visited by two sovereigns. Charles I came in 1625 (accompanied by the Duke of Buckingham), soon after his accession to the throne; and William of Orange made it his first, or second, sleeping-place (some ascribe priority to Paignton, and others assert that priority goes to Brixham itself) after leaving Brixham, when on his way to London to assume the government of the kingdom. The bedroom he occupied at Forde is still pointed out. His army was encamped on Milber Down, close by; and his first proclamation was read by the rector of Wolborough, the Rev. John Reynell, from the stump of the old market cross—according to the inscription on it—at the east end of Wolborough Street, in front of St. Leonard's Tower. The date is given as November 5th, but it should be the 6th or 7th. Fairfax apparently passed one night at Forde, and it is more than possible that Cromwell was with him.

Newton Abbot has some interesting buildings. **Wolborough Church** is situated on a slope, from which may be seen some of the tors of Dartmoor. It is in the Perpendicular style, with a fine rood-screen, a noteworthy Reynell tomb, and a fireplace in the south porch; the font is Norman. The decay of the ancient framework prevented the bells from being rung, and in 1926, through the munificence of several Newtonians, the three old bells were recast with their old inscriptions and a full peal of eight completed. One of the old bells, weighing $15\frac{3}{4}$ cwts., is exhibited in the church. The rarest possession of the church is the old brass eagle lectern, one of fifty such left in the churches of England. Opposite the lych gate is a good path which, passing the Mackrell Almshouses, leads to Wolborough Street and the centre of the town, conspicuous objects of which are the **Market Place** and **St. Leonard's Tower,** about 60 feet high, all that was spared in the demolition of the old church of St. Leonard in 1834. The new church stands about 300 yards away.

Highweek Church, on a commanding site, is a Perpendicular building dating from early in the fifteenth century, but it was sadly mutilated during alterations in 1786 and now shows little of interest save one memorial to the Yardes, a few fragments of old glass, and an old wagon-roof. From the churchyard a wide-spreading view up the Teign Valley towards Haldon is obtained.

The Newton Abbot **College of Art** and the **Public Library** form a fine block at the corner of Highweek and Market Streets. Passmore Edwards defrayed the cost of the Library as a memorial to his mother, a native of Newton Abbot. The **Hospital** in East Street may be mentioned as being originally the scene of early researches into the cure of cancer by means of radium.

Visitors may tour the **New Devon Pottery and Devon**

Leathercraft factories in Forde Road to see all stages of manufacture (*Easter to October, guided tours, Monday to Friday 9.30–12, 1.30–4.30; charge*).

To the west of the town off the Totnes road stands **Bradley Manor** in a beautiful peaceful setting in the valley of the Lemon. It is one of the oldest inhabited houses in Devon and is now owned by the National Trust (*open Easter to September, Wednesdays 2–5 and at other times on written application*). Mostly fifteenth century, and incorporating an earlier house of the thirteenth century, this home is a good specimen of a small manor-house of the West Country type. It has a chapel of Perpendicular architecture. The house was originally quadrangular, but two sides were pulled down in the eighteenth century. Some of the rooms contain good plaster work, and over the fireplace of the old guest chamber are the arms of the Yarde family, one of whom obtained, in 1428, a licence for the chapel, which possesses a wagon-roof with carved bosses. In the porch is the wheel of the ill-fated *Herzogin Cecilie*, wrecked on the Ham Stone near Bolt Head in 1936.

Excursions from Newton Abbot

1. To Teignmouth

Leave Newton Abbot by the A380 Exeter road and at Kingsteignton turn right along the A381. A turning on the left leads to—

Bishopsteignton

The village lies under the height of Haldon (800 feet). It owes the "teignton" part of its name to its position near the River Teign. Its prefix is believed to have been bestowed because Bishop Brones-combe of Exeter, lord of the manor from 1258 to 1280, erected a palace here, portions of the walls of the chapel attached to which are still in existence—in the lane leading from Ash Hill to the Teign-mouth–Exeter high road on Haldon.

Bishopsteignton Church is an old foundation, largely rebuilt in 1815. The western doorway and font are Norman, and good speci-mens of that style. Outside, on the south wall, is a carving of very early design and considered unique, representing the Adoration of the Magi. In the churchyard are ruins of a sanctuary chapel built by Bishop Grandisson (1327–1369).

Bishopsteignton lies about 2½ miles from—

Teignmouth

Bathing.—Excellent, but swimmers should keep away from the estuary.
Bowls.—Public greens on the Den and in Bitton Park.
Buses.—To Newton Abbot, Dawlish, Exeter and Torbay.
Cinema.—*Riviera*, Den Crescent.
Early Closing.—Thursday.
Ferry.—Motor ferry to Shaldon starting from near the old Lifeboat House.
Fishing.—Bass, pollack etc., and in the season good mackerel fishing in the bay. Salmon and trout in the Teign.

Golf.—*Teignmouth Golf Club* on Little Haldon.
Population.—13,220.
Sailing.—During the season a programme of regattas and sailing events is arranged.
Tennis.—Public courts on the Den.
Theatre.—*Carlton Theatre*.
Zoo.—Children's Zoo and Pets' Corner at the Ness, Shaldon.

Situated on a triangular plateau under the lee of one of the spurs of Haldon, Teignmouth is bounded on the south-east by the English Channel, while on the south-west is the broad, sandy estuary of the River Teign. Where one's eye, in glancing round the town, does not rest on water there are wooded hills, which effectually shelter it from the north and north-east. Indeed, the inhabitants set great store by the situation of their town and its climate. Teignmouth is pleasant at most times of the year, and is usually warm in the winter.

The Sea-Front and Den

The chief attractions of Teignmouth are its sea front, the River Teign, and the varied beauties of the surrounding country. Facing the sea is the **Den,** six acres of green turf forming a delightful marine promenade, and laid out with flower beds, rockeries, paths and shelters. On the Den, too, is the **War Memorial,** an obelisk of granite. At the northern end is the *Carlton Theatre* and a public bowling green, and towards the southern end a putting course and tennis courts. A well-stocked Aquarium is a further attraction.

Why this pleasant stretch of greensward is called the Den is not very certain. One theory is that the word is derived from the familiar *dune*, a hill, on the ground that the Den was once a barren stretch of sand hills or dunes.

Teignmouth has for long been famous for its bathing. The sand is coarse but firm and shelves gradually.

The Sea-Wall Promenade

The seaward front of Teignmouth offers the attraction of a well-surfaced sea-walk of two miles. From where the Den at its southern end is washed by the waters of the Teign as they flow under the Ness (the great red sandstone headland on the fringe of which Shaldon has been built) to Hole Head on the north, is a dry, level walk. Where the Den ends at the north-east, there begins almost immediately a terraced walk under the shadow of the cliffs, at the base of which tamarisk and other shrubs have been planted to lend additional shelter to the seats. Beyond the point where the railway runs from the town to the edge of the sea under the **Cliff Bridge,** leading to Holcombe and Dawlish, there is a sea-wall, the trains being on one side and the sea on the other. The sea-walk terminates at **Hole Head,** where the railway leaps the little cove at the foot of Smugglers' Lane. Walkers can vary the return route by proceeding up this pretty lane to the Dawlish and Teignmouth road, and thence (by taking Cliff Road to the left) returning to Teignmouth along a narrow lane and over the Cliff Bridge.

The Town
At the southern end of the Den are the ferry to Shaldon and boats for fishing, rowing or sailing. Near the extreme point is the **Lighthouse,** the red lamp of which operates in connection with a similar one on the front of Powderham Terrace. Here, too, is the principal public car park.

Proceeding inland *via* the Strand, Northumberland Place, and Fore Street, one arrives at the parish church of West Teignmouth, **St. James's Church,** a heavy, battlemented octagonal building, its interior presenting a peculiar appearance on account of the slender pillars supporting the roof, in the centre of which is an octagonal lantern. The reredos is a beautiful specimen of fourteenth-century stone carving. It is Perpendicular in style, with exquisite little figures of saints under canopies surmounted by delicate pinnacles and finials. The Commandments were painted later. The tower on the western side of the octagon is all that remains of the structure mentioned in Bishop Bronescombe's Register, dated 1275. The bells in it are said to have been rung after the battle of Crécy, 1346; but they were recast in 1879.

A quarter of a mile west of the church is the pleasant open space of **Bitton Park.** This consists of five acres of well-kept and sheltered gardens at the west end of the town, a little short of the bridge, and overlooking the river. The Park formed part of the old Bitton estate, once the seat of that Lord Exmouth famed in connection with the bombardment of Algiers, at that time a stronghold of the Barbary pirates.

The return to Newton Abbot may be made by crossing the Teign to Shaldon and following the B3195 through **Combeteignhead.** For a detailed description of places on the south bank of the river see the *Red Guide to South Devon*.

2. To Bovey Tracey and Chagford
Leave Newton Abbot by the A382 Okehampton road which leads in 6 miles to—

Bovey Tracey

This small but rapidly growing town is a good centre for excursions in the eastern fringes of Dartmoor. It lies beside the little River Bovey which flows into the Teign lower down. From it there are beautiful views of Haytor and the Moor. The mainly fifteenth-century **Church** replaced one built by Sir William Tracy but later burnt down. It is notable for its richly carved rood-screen, stone pulpit, chancel miserichords and fourteenth-century tower.

For a walk in the area, see page 106.

In a further 3 miles a left turn leads to **Lustleigh** where the most notable buildings are the church with screen dating from the reign of Queen Mary and the delightful fifteenth-century *Cleave Inn*. To the west the charming scenery of **Lustleigh Cleave** above the Bovey attracts many walkers (see page 108).

Continue along the main road through Moretonhampstead (see page 48) and in 3 miles turn left for—

Chagford

"Chaggyford", as the natives call it, is an old market town once important for tin mining and cloth working. It was formerly one of the Stannary towns, the special places where tin had to be weighed and stamped. It is a favourite headquarters for Dartmoor visitors, for here all tastes can be gratified, anglers being provided with good fishing in the Teign, antiquaries with a boundless field for their inspection and investigation, lovers of scenery with the glorious Teign Gorge, and the lover of the Moor with access to some of the wildest as well as to most of the more familiar parts of it.

The town consists of a few irregularly-built streets that branch off from a Square, in the centre of which is the **Market House**. The **Church** is well situated, and is an Early Perpendicular building of Dartmoor granite. It contains a monument of Sir John Whyddon, who died in 1575, a member of an ancient family now extinct, whose name survives in Whiddon Park and Whiddon Down.

For walks in the area, see page 95.

For the return journey to Newton Abbot leave Chagford by the road running directly southward and in ½ mile take a left fork. The road crosses the Moretonhampstead–Princetown road and continues as the B3344 to **Manaton**. The village green beside the church is a place of peace and the interior of the church itself is notable for the finely carved screen running right across it. Just off the main road about a mile to the south are **Becky Falls** which are well worth seeing after a heavy fall of rain.

The B3344 joins the A382 Okehampton–Newton Abbot road just south-west of Bovey Tracey. An attractive detour may be preferred. A right turn where the road comes nearest to Becky Falls leads to Haytor Vale close to Haytor (1,490 feet) and on to **Ilsington**. The typical moorland church here has a damaged but still rich rood-screen.

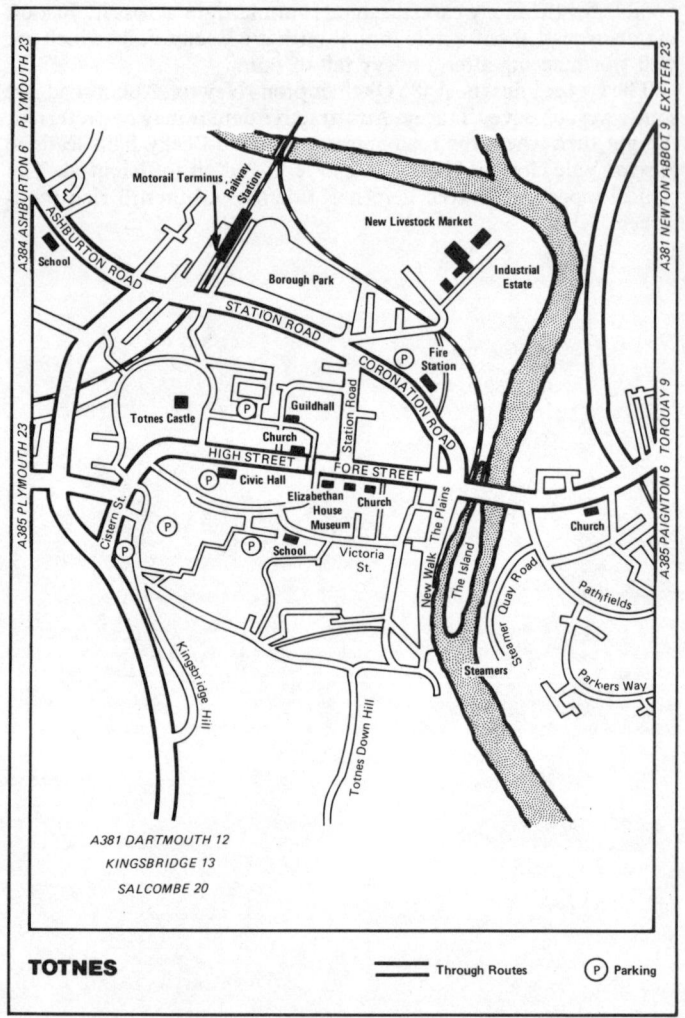

A381 DARTMOUTH 12
KINGSBRIDGE 13
SALCOMBE 20

TOTNES ═══ Through Routes Ⓟ Parking

Totnes

Bowls.—Borough Park.

Distances.—Exeter, 25 miles; Kingsbridge, 14; London, 197; Paignton, 6; Plymouth, 24.

Early Closing.—Thursday.

Fishing.—Rod and line fishing for salmon and trout. Licences and information from the Clerk to the Dart District Fishery Board, Totnes. For fishing between Totnes and Buckfastleigh, the Dart Angling Association licence must be obtained.

Market Day.—Friday (Pannier); cattle markets every Tuesday.

Population.—5,830.

Tennis.—Grass and hard courts in Borough Park.

History

Totnes is one of the most charming of old towns. Legend dates its history from 1170 B.C., for a tradition repeated by Geoffrey of Monmouth assures us that Brutus the Trojan, the reputed colonizer of Britain, landed at this spot, when the Dart was an inlet of the Channel and its waters laved the hill on which the old town stood; and the inhabitants point with pride to the **Brutus Stone,** a granite block sunk into the pavement just above No. 51 Fore Street (a sign is placed in the wall above it), as proving the truth of this assertion. The name "Brutus", however, is probably a corruption of Bruiter's or Town Crier's Stone. The stone at one time projected 18 inches above the pavement, but was levelled in the interests of traffic. The Mayor still stands upon it on the proclamation of a new sovereign.

Totnes claims to be one of the oldest boroughs in the kingdom. Saxon coins minted at Totnes were found during excavations at the castle. As coins were only minted in fortified towns, Totnes, in the tenth century, was probably a small settlement covering about 10 acres, and surrounded by earthen ramparts, which were replaced later by stone walls. In the eleventh century, William the Conqueror bestowed this royal *burh* on Judhael—the reputed founder of Totnes Castle (see p. 71).

Totnes was an important town when the Normans subjugated England, for we find from Domesday Book that it was held by

Judhael direct from the King; that there were "within the borough one hundred burgesses, less five, and fifteen without the borough, working the land" and that it was only taxed when Exeter was taxed. "If an expedition sets out by land or by sea," the entry goes on, "Totenais, Barnstaple, and Lideford (Lydford) render between them as much service as Exeter renders." In 1206, King John granted the town its first charter and it possesses the original roll of the Guild merchants, said to be the oldest in existence. The list of mayors dates from 1331; the public ceremony of swearing in the mayor is held annually at the Guildhall.

Totnes quay has been in use for nearly a thousand years. The Saxons used the port, and there was probably some overseas trade. The height of its importance was between the fourteenth and seventeenth centuries, when large quantities of wool and cloth were exported and Totnes merchants grew very wealthy. Trade declined, and the harbour silted up. Constant dredging is now necessary to enable the chief industry of the town—the importation of timber from northern Europe—to be carried on.

Totnes Grammar School was founded in 1553 by Edward VI and has produced many notable men. Among them may be mentioned Benjamin Kennicott, whose Hebrew Bible was published in 1776; Sir William Whiteway, who became a Premier of Newfoundland; and Charles Babbage, the mathematician. Other eminent men born in Totnes are Edward Lye, the Saxon grammarian and compiler of the dictionary of that language; William Brockedon, author, painter, and Alpine traveller; and the Earl of Totnes, who made his mark in the Irish wars of Queen Elizabeth I's time. On a granite **Obelisk,** in front of the *Royal Seven Stars Hotel*, in the Plains, is recorded that it was erected "In honour of William John Wills, native of Totnes, the first, with Burke to cross the Australian continent; he perished in returning, 28 June, 1861." Among the names of distinguished freemen is that of the well-known soldier Lord Birdwood of Anzac and Totnes.

Round the Town

The best approach for the visitor to the town is from the bridge which spans the river, a short distance from the spot where the steamer lands passengers from Dartmouth. The landing-place is very near to what is known as the **Island,** reached from the bridge, a delightfully shady riverside pleasure-ground, laid out for the enjoyment of the townspeople by a former Duke of Somerset. The bridge is the boundary between the parishes of Totnes and **Bridgetown,** its less important neighbour. The view from this point, up the steep hill which the town's chief thoroughfare climbs laboriously—passing beneath the quaint old East Gate which spans the roadway—suggests something of the antiquarian and historical interest which this old town excites.

On The Quay near the Bridge is the **Totnes Motor Museum** (*Easter to October, daily 10–6*), a private collection of cars many of which are in everyday use for both travel and racing. It specializes in vintage, sports and racing cars.

Totnes is one of the few places where the curfew bell is still rung and where, in addition, a day bell is rung early every morning—an ancient call to prayers.

During the summer Totnes is particularly busy on Tuesdays. Visitors flock to see the townspeople dressed up in Elizabethan costume making a most colourful scene against a background of buildings some of which are of that period.

The town is one of the chief gateways to the South Hams. It was spoken of by Camden as a "little town hanging from east to west on the side of a hill"—a description which still holds good. Of old, it was defended by a strong castle, and was surrounded by walls which may still be traced, and which show that it was then much smaller, so tiny that it must have been one of the smallest walled towns in the kingdom. There were in the wall four gates, opening to the cardinal points of the compass. Of these, two remain, the **North** and **East Gates.** In Fore Street, not far above the Brutus Stone, is an Elizabethan house in which is the **Totnes Museum** (*April–September, weekdays*). Nearby is the **East Gate** which spans the roadway and divides Fore Street from High Street. It has been greatly altered of late years; but of old it consisted of two arched portals, one for carriages, which was enclosed with gates, and a smaller one, "a needle's eye", for foot passengers. The clock, with a face for each side of the arch, was added in 1878. On the east side is an oriel window.

Stone steps lead from the East Gate to Rampart Walk, a narrow road which follows the line of the old walls past the church and Guildhall to the stone arched North Gate.

The **Parish Church of St. Mary's** is a grand and impressive red sandstone edifice of the fifteenth century, in the Perpendicular style, with a massive square tower surmounted by crocketed pinnacles. Halfway up are three niches containing statuettes. It is known from a charter of Judhael de Totenaes in 1088 that there was a church here, and from the deeds of Totnes Priory it is evident that soon after that date a Priory Church was built to the north-east of the present church, and other buildings erected in connection with the Benedictine Priory, the only remains of which are now the Guildhall and, in part, a private house called "The Priory". The Priory Church and the parish church were united in 1259, and in the first half of the fifteenth century the parish church was rebuilt. The church was restored (1867–1879) by Sir G. G. Scott. The rood-screen, with two parclose screens of Beer stone, is one of the finest stone screens in England, but the loft was removed at the restoration. Other objects of interest are the Corporation seats bearing the town arms, a Bible and Prayer Book (both at the west end of the north aisle), presented to the church for the use of the mayor by Lady Ann Seymour, in 1690, together with the Indulgence granted by Bishop Lacy mentioned above, and an altar cloth of 1682; two handsome candelabras, dated 1701 and 1732; and some interesting tombs.

Opposite the church, Barclays Bank is housed in an old building (No. 16) bearing the date 1585, and lower down the initials N.B., standing for Nicholas Ball, one time mayor and M.P. Thomas Bodley, the founder of the famous Library at Oxford, married the rich widow of Ball in 1586.

The **Guildhall** (*Easter to September, Monday to Friday 9.30–1, 2–5, Saturday 10–12; October to March by appointment*) stands to the north of the church and is one of the most interesting municipal buildings in the west of England. It occupied part of the site of St. Mary's Priory, founded about 1088 by Judhael. After the dissolution of the monasteries the land was granted to the Corporation, and the present Guildhall, which dates from the sixteenth and seventeenth centuries, was built on the site.

In the main hall are displayed the old stocks, a man-trap and the old bull ring in addition to several paintings of local interest. At one side is the doorway of the old lock-up. The Council Chamber is a low room, the ceiling sloping up to a large skylight, and with old oaken stalls for the Mayor and Corporation, and a fine plaster frieze, with the town arms and date, 1624, over the fireplace. In the Guildhall are kept many of the valuable records of Totnes. Adjoining the Guildhall is the original site of the Grammar School, which is now in Fore Street.

A few steps from the church, and near the North Gate of the town, are the well preserved ruins of Totnes **Castle** (*March and October, weekdays 9.30–5.30, Sunday 2–5.30; April, daily 9.30–5.30; May to September, weekdays 9.30–7, Sunday 2–7; November to February, weekdays 9.30–4, Sunday 2–4*). The circular keep with walls 15 feet thick occupies a lofty mound from the top of which there are extensive views.

The Castle is generally believed to have been founded by Judhael de Totenais, the Norman knight to whom the Conqueror gave the manor, but this is uncertain, and Hooker inclines to the belief that "it was buylded either by the inhabitants of the same for the defence of theymselffes and of their towne when before the Conquest the Danes and fforeyn enemyes used invasions and exercysed great cruelties as well in this west countrie as yn other places of the lande, or by someone of the lordes, and for their command of the towne did buyld the same".

Near the Castle, at the bend in the High Street, is the site of the **West Gate,** demolished at the beginning of the nineteenth century. Just beyond are two colonnades known as **Butterwalk** and **Poultry Walk.** The upper storeys of the buildings project over the pavement, and are supported by pillars, thus providing a picturesque covered walk. Before the market was built, poultry and farm products were displayed and sold in the sheltered *piazzas*—hence the names. In High Street and Fore Street are several sixteenth- and seventeenth-century houses, many of them possessing richly decorated plaster ceilings. Others have the typical Devon slate-hung fronts. In byways and lanes are other reminders of Totnes's antiquity. A Leper House once stood in Maudlin Road and the narrow footpath connecting it with Leechwell Lane is still referred to as "Leper's Way". Yet, steeped in history and tradition as it is, Totnes does not rest on past achievements. It is a thriving centre with excellent shops and a busy market. It is an attractive holiday resort, and is rapidly developing light industries.

Excursions from Totnes

Totnes is the centre of a lovely district (with good bus services in all directions) within 10 miles of the resorts of Torbay and on the threshold of the Dartmoor National Park. Walkers can easily explore the sequestered villages and ridges with spreading views bordering the River Dart.

1. To Dartington Hall

The Dartington Hall estate lies in a large bend of the Dart about 1 mile north of Totnes. The fourteenth-century manor house, built by John Holland, half-brother of Richard II, is an interesting example of careful restoration. The estate is now a Trust with agricultural and commercial enterprises formed into several companies. Endowed departments are Dartington College of Arts (including the Devon Centre for Further Education sponsored by the Devon Education Authority), a co-educational boarding school and the Adult Education Centre. In the garden the fine trees and flowering shrubs, and the terraces overlooking the old tiltyard are of particular interest. The estate is private property, but the gardens and Hall (if not in use) may be visited without appointment (no coaches).

The walk may be extended by following the Ashburton road from Dartington Church to Huxham's Cross. From here a descent through the woods emerges by the lovely old bridge which spans the Dart at Staverton. The return may be made by the Totnes bus.

Another delightful walk from Dartington Church is to the beautiful old village of **Rattery,** reached by turning left at Huxham Cross. The church is a thirteenth-century building with fifteenth-century additions; it has a fine Norman font and fifteenth-century screens. Adjoining the church is one of England's oldest inns, the eleventh-century *Church House Inn.*

Dartington Hall

72

2. To Ashburton and Widecombe-in-the-Moor

Leave Totnes by the A385 Plymouth road and in 1 mile fork right along the A384. This joins the reconstructed A38 Plymouth–Exeter trunk road which in about 3 miles by-passes—

Ashburton

This peaceful residential town, once a Stannary town well known for cloth manufacturing, is beautifully situated in lovely countryside. Some of the most attractive parts of Dartmoor are within comparatively easy reach.

The town has a number of typical Devon gabled houses, some about three hundred years old. The Church is Late Decorated and Perpendicular in period with a fine west tower decorated with niches for statues. But the architect G. E. Street in an over-enthusiastic reconstruction did away with the original rood-screen which was the church's chief claim to distinction.

The **Ashburton Museum** (*mid-May to September, Tuesday, Thursday, Friday and Saturday 2.30–5, free*) houses collections of local antiquities, costumes, tools, geological specimens and exhibits relating to the American Indians.

Just outside the town on the B3357 Dartmoor road the **River Dart Country Park** (*daily 10–6*) comprises 8 acres of river, lakes and parkland where nature and forest trails, an adventure wood and fishing facilities are available for visitors.

About 2 miles north of Asburton is **Buckland-in-the-Moor** just below the meeting of the East and West Webburn rivers. There are some beautiful walks along the wooded slopes of the valley. The village itself is pretty and unspoilt, including some delightful thatched cottages. The little church, notable for its richly painted screen, is mainly of the fifteenth and sixteenth centuries, but the south doorway and font date from the twelfth. A 3-mile drive northward close to the East Webburn brings one to—

Widecombe-in-the-Moor

Visitors flock in the summer to Widecombe, long famous for its church and for the fair held on the second Tuesday in September and immortalized in the song "Uncle Tom Cobleigh". The village is superbly set against a background of bleak moors and is best enjoyed after the coaches have departed.

Buckland-in-the-Moor

The **Church,** often called the "cathedral of the Moor", is notable for its magnificent 120-feet-high granite tower, which is said to have been erected by the tinners who prospered there in the early sixteenth century. A board at the west end of the spacious interior records an occasion in 1638 when the church was struck by lightning with the loss of several lives. There are some interesting bosses in the chancel ceiling. Outside the church is the long stone **Church House** dating from about 1500 and owned by the National Trust.

There are many interesting antiquities in the surrounding countryside including remains of medieval villages which may well have been deserted at the time of the Black Death, hut circles and rocking stones. For walks and rides in the area, see page 108.

3. To Buckfast Abbey and Dartmeet
Follow the route described in the previous excursion but at the A38 turn left for—

Buckfastleigh

This small market town has few buildings of interest though the **Church,** built in the thirteenth century, has a fine Norman font and fifteenth-century screens.

On the other side of the main road by the banks of the Dart is the terminus of the privately operated **Dart Valley Railway** which runs its beautiful course by the riverside to Totnes (no access to the town). The trains, which run several times daily in the summer, are hauled by steam locomotives. Several superb examples of Great Western Railway rolling stock are on display at the station. There is also a miniature railway.

About 2 miles south-west of Buckfastleigh is the parish of **Dean Prior,** of which the poet Herrick was vicar. He was presented to the living in 1629, and held it for eighteen years, when he was ejected by the Puritan supremacy. He returned to Dean Prior at the Restoration in 1662 and lived here until his death at eighty-three. The registers contain a record of the burial of "Robert Herrick vicker", October 15, 1674. There is a modern brass tablet to his memory in the church, and in 1926 there was unveiled in the chancel a very beautiful window dedicated to his memory.

Dean Court—passed *en route* to Dean Prior—now a farmhouse, was the Tudor mansion of the Giles family, and was built in Edward VI's reign. It has an interesting old hall, decorated with trophies of the chase. Sir Edward Giles (*d.* 1642) and family have an interesting monument in Dean Prior church.

Reached from the Dart Bridge at the junction of the A38 and A384 is—

Buckfast Abbey

Open free all year: Sunday 11.45–6.15, weekdays 9–6.15 except during services.

A Saxon abbey was founded here in 1018 by Ethelward, an ealdorman of King Canute, and was generously endowed by the king himself. The tradition that a Celtic foundation had existed on the spot before Canute's time is no longer admitted. In 1147 Buckfast Abbey was affiliated to the Cistercian Order, to which it remained attached until the Dissolution under Henry VIII in 1539. From that time onwards the buildings were gradually dismantled. A modern house built on the site in 1806 completed the destruction of

Buckfast Abbey

the old abbey, but in 1882 a group of French Benedictine monks bought the place with a view to its complete restoration. The Abbey church was rebuilt by the monks themselves, to the plans and under the direction of the late Fred A. Walters, a London architect. This rebuilding, started in 1906 by Abbot Anscar Vonier and a few Brothers, was completed in December 1938. Only the structural work was carried out by the monks themselves; the altars, stalls, windows, etc., were produced by secular professionals. Splendid examples of metal work, executed at Aix-la-Chapelle by the world's leading goldsmiths, are to be seen on the high altar, the font and Stations of the Cross. The Memorial plaque to Abbot Vonier, who was buried in the church by special privilege, was the work of the late Benno Elkan. In 1960 Buckfast Abbey was affiliated to the English Benedictine Congregation, to which Downside and Ampleforth also belong. In 1965 a new Blessed Sacrament Chapel was added. The stained glass, a conspicuous feature, was carried out by the monks. In 1967 a small preparatory school was inaugurated, the teaching staff being made up of the Abbey monks.

77

Dartmeet from Comberstone Tor

Adjoining the Abbey the **House of Shells** (*Easter to October, daily 10–7*) houses a museum of shell craft with exhibits from many parts of the world, some dating from the eighteenth century.

From the Abbey follow the road skirting **Hembury Castle**, an Iron Age hill-fort known locally as Danes' Camp and set in the midst of 327 acres of National Trust property. It stands above Holy Brook, 2 miles north of Buckfastleigh.

Continue north-westward to **Holne,** where the church has a fine screen with well preserved paintings and a carved pulpit both of the fifteenth century. Charles Kingsley the novelist was born at the vicarage in 1819 when his father was the incumbent.

Beyond Holne the road skirts **Venford Reservoir** with splendid views over wild moorland to the west and the softer Dart valley to the east. Negotiating the narrow bridge at **Hexworthy** with difficulty, we reach the B3357 Ashburton–Tavistock road. To the left it leads in 3 miles to Two Bridges (see page 49). However we turn right arriving in ½ mile at romantically beautiful **Dartmeet** where the East and West Dart rivers unite. For a walk in the area, see page 122.

The main road continues through Poundsgate to join the A38 just outside Ashburton.

4. To Harberton and South Brent
Leave Totnes by the A381 Kingsbridge road and in about 1 mile turn right for—

Harberton
This village is notable for its church whose outstanding feature is the great fifteenth-century rood-screen. Partly restored in the Victorian period, it stretches across the church resplendent with carvings and coloured in gold, blue, green and red. The fine stone pulpit is adorned with carvings of the apostles executed in the seventeenth century.

The road continues westward, in 4 miles joining the B3210 at **Avonwick** on the River Avon. Turn left, then shortly fork right for—

South Brent
This typical moorland town lies just north of the A38 trunk road. Its spring fair and pony market no longer enjoy the importance that they once had. The weather-beaten **Church** is in the Perpendicular and Decorated styles with a low Norman tower which originally was a central tower, the old west end having been destroyed. There is a Norman font and piscinae in the chancel and south transept. Fragments of a former screen are incorporated in the altar rails and form the base of a war memorial.

On the moors to the north-west are many vestiges of barrows, hut circles and other evidences of Bronze Age civilization.

Plymouth

Association Football.—Plymouth Argyle play in the Football League at Home Park.

Beach Huts.—For hire at Tinside, Pebbleside, Hoe Foreshore and Devil's Point.

Bowls.—Public greens at The Hoe, Tothill Park, Central Park, North Down, St. Budeaux, Devonport Park, Victoria Park, Plympton and Dean Cross, Plymstock.

Cinemas.—*A.B.C. 1, 2, 3; Belgrave; Drake; Odeon; Plaza.*

Distances.—Bodmin, 30 miles; Exeter, 44; Kingsbridge, 21; London, 216; Tavistock, 15; Torquay, 36.

Early Closing.—Wednesday.

Fishing.—Excellent sea fishing both from the shore and from boats readily available for hire, the deep-water marks of Eddystone and Hand Deeps being famous. Contact the Plymouth Sea Anglers Club. Trout fishing on Burrator Reservoir: permits and boats obtainable on site. Day tickets may be obtained for stretches on many rivers within easy reach.

Golf.—18-hole courses at Yelverton and Stadden Heights, 9-hole-course at Elfordleigh, Plympton. Miniature golf course in Central Park.

Greyhound Racing.—Pennycross Stadium.

Library, Museum and Art Gallery.—Drake Circus.

Population.—249,800.

Swimming Pools.—Open-air pools at Tinside and Mount Wise. Heated indoor pool in Central Park.

Tennis.—Courts at Westhoe Recreation Ground, Freedom Park, Tothill Recreation Ground, Hartley Recreation Ground, Central Park, Devonport Park, Plympton and Plymstock.

Theatres.—*Hoe* (summer shows, repertory), *Athenaeum* (repertory, ballet).

Tourist Information Centre.—Civic Centre.

Zoo.—Central Park.

The city of Plymouth lies at the mouth of the River Tamar which here forms the boundary between Devon and Cornwall. It faces on to Plymouth Sound, a great expanse of water almost 3 miles square. The city incorporates the formerly separate townships of Devonport, Stonehouse and old Plymouth and with a population of 250,000 is the largest centre in the West Country.

The foreshore is shaped like a great bow and extends for a distance of 7 miles from the point where the River Plym becomes the Cattewater, the old commercial harbour, round the shore of Plymouth Sound and up the Hamoaze, the great naval anchorage, to beyond the fine road bridge across the Tamar.

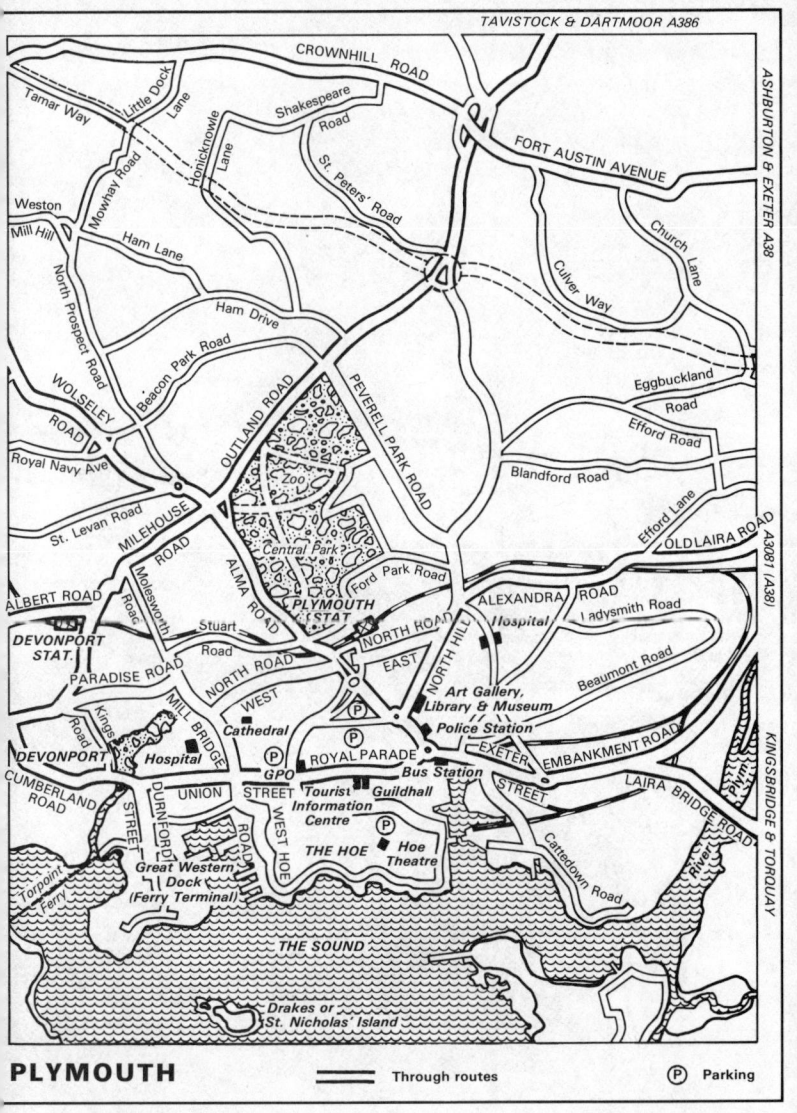

PLYMOUTH

━━━ Through routes   ℗ Parking

Overleaf Custom House and Sutton Harbour

The **Hoe,** 120 feet above sea-level, is one of the finest promenades in Europe. The broad asphalted plateau is about a quarter of a mile in length. On the seaward side it slopes down to the rocks which form the barrier of the waters of the Sound, while townwards it drops gently through lawns and gardens fringed with trees. The Sound, as seen from the Hoe, is a constant theatre of maritime activity with all manner of vessels from giant naval warships to tiny rowboats gracefully pursuing their ways. The Hoe is, of course, famous in history for it was here that Drake finished his game of bowls despite the approach of the Spanish Armada.

The **Armada Memorial** is only one of several on the Hoe. The statue of Sir Francis Drake is by Boehm—there is a duplicate at Tavistock. The **Naval War Memorial,** a lofty obelisk designed by Sir Robert Lorimer, serves also as a sea mark for ships entering the Sound. On the townward slope is Hoe Park with bowling greens and putting, and at the entrance the War Memorial. **Smeaton's Lighthouse** (*May to September, daily 10–8*) stands boldly on the grassy slopes. It first stood on the Eddystone rock for a hundred and twenty years before being replaced by the present structure on an adjacent rock. The old lighthouse was taken down and re-erected here. Eastward in a railed enclosure is a beautifully kept little garden and nearby the **Hoe Theatre** built in 1962.

The **Royal Citadel** (*mid-April to September, daily conducted tours at 2, 3, 4 and 5*) is a picturesque fortification built in the time of Charles II. The gateway on the inland side is beautified with fine carving. Many of the original buildings have been replaced and additions made but the walls are most impressive. In front is the **Aquarium** (*weekdays 10–6*) of the Marine Biological Association.

Sutton Pool is the ancient harbour of Plymouth, lined with quays and stores. Beyond Phoenix Wharf is the old Barbican, a point of great historic interest. On the West Pier is the famous **Mayflower Stone** commemorating the departure from this spot of the Pilgrim Fathers on 6 September, 1620. There are many quaint old buildings nearby. At Guy's Quay is moored the **Kathleen and May** (*daily 10–6*), the last of the wooden topsail schooners to trade from the west country. The National Maritime Museum has mounted an exhibition in the hold.

At No. 32 New Street is the **Elizabethan House** (*April to September, weekdays 10–1, 2.15–6, Sunday 3–5; October to March,* *weekdays only 10–1, 2.15–dusk*). This survival from the sixteenth century is filled with Elizabethan and Jacobean furniture and has a delightful courtyard and gardens.

At No. 60 Southside Street, forming part of a distillery is **Black Friars Refectory Room** (*May to August, Monday to Friday 10.30–1, 2–4.30; free*), an ancient building at which the Pilgrim Fathers reputedly held their final meeting before sailing to America.

From the Barbican Southside Street and High Street lead to Whimple Street and so to **St. Andrew's Church,** the parish church, rebuilt in 1957 after almost total destruction in the war. It has a Piper window of interest. Immediately behind the church, off Royal Parade, is **Prysten House** (*Monday to Saturday 10–4*), the former priest's house of St. Andrew's built in 1490. It houses the new Plymouth Tapestry and a Mayflower exhibition.

At No. 33 St. Andrew's Street is the recently restored **Merchant's House** (*weekdays 10–1, 2.15–6, Sunday 3–5*). This large town house dating from the sixteenth and early seventeenth centuries houses the Plymouth History Museum.

The **City Museum and Art Gallery** (*Monday to Thursday and Saturday 10–6, Friday 10–8, Sunday 3–5; free*) is located at Drake Circus. There are extensive collections of English and foreign paintings and drawings, porcelain, silver and early books and manuscripts. There are also exhibits relating to local history, archaeology and natural history.

Of great moment to Plymouth has been the rebuilding of the city centre, wiped out by the devastating air raids of 1941. An ambitious and farseeing plan was evolved and has been carried out speedily and with commendable success. It involves a shopping community surrounded by an inner ring road, well landscaped with gardens and floral displays and permitting a direct pedestrian route, now Armada Way, from the rail centre to the sea. Several traffic-free precincts have been included.

The fine **Guildhall** was badly damaged but a new complex has been built within the old walls, whilst close by are the new Law Courts and the Police Station. Opposite rises the new **Civic Centre,** a mammoth modern building from the roof of which (*Monday to Saturday 10–4.30*) there is a wonderful prospect over the city and the sea.

Excursions from Plymouth

Plymouth is an ideal centre for visiting the southern coasts of both Devon and Cornwall being situated very near the county border. There are *Red Guides* to South Devon and South Cornwall. But Plymouth is also a convenient centre for touring Dartmoor.

1. To Yelverton and Princetown

Leave Plymouth by the A386 Tavistock road. About 1 mile beyond Plymouth Airport a right turn leads to **Bickleigh** where an old bridge crosses the River Plym which here runs through the beautiful wooded Bickleigh Vale. The church is notable for its pinnacled tower and its two fonts, one of the fifteenth century, the other much older.

A road runs northward close to the Plym, crossing it at its junction with the Meavy where the National Trust owns much of the lovely surroundings. **Shaugh Prior** was the home of the Devon poet Noel Carrington. The font in the church has an oaken cover 8 feet high and strikingly carved. Keep left after the village for **Cadover Bridge,** a good centre for exploring a large number of Bronze Age remains. Just to the north the hamlet of **Brisworthy** was one of the earliest tin works, mentioned in 1168.

At **Cadover Bridge** the left turn leads to Yelverton, while the road to the right forms part of the western boundary of the National Park and runs past china clay workings to Cornwood and Ivybridge (see page 92).

The main A386 road continues to **Yelverton,** now little more than a dormitory suburb of Plymouth though visitors enjoy the golf course and good fishing in four nearby rivers, the Meavy, Cad (Plym), Walkham and Tavy. The church, in the style of the fourteenth century, is modern.

Two miles west of Yelverton is **Buckland Abbey** (*Easter to September, weekdays 11–6, Sunday 2–6; October to Easter, Wednesday,*

Sheepstor and Burrator Reservoir

Saturday and Sunday 3–5). This National Trust property is a thirteenth-century monastic foundation subsequently given by Henry VIII to Sir Richard Grenville, grandfather of Richard Grenville of the "Revenge", and later bought by Sir Francis Drake. It is now a naval and Devon folk museum with Grenville and Drake relics.

The church in the village of **Buckland Monachorum** to the north has both a Saxon and a Norman font. The Drake aisle contains monuments to members of the Drake family. Outside the village the **Garden House** is well known to horticulturists for its lawns, terraces, trees and shrubs (*gardens open mid-April to early September, Wednesday 3–7*).

From Yelverton the A386 continues to Tavistock while the B3212 runs north-eastward across the Moor to Princetown 6 miles distant. At the crossroads reached in about 1 mile the left turn leads to **Walkhampton** whose hill-top church with fifteenth-century tower is a landmark for miles around. The right turn leads to **Meavy,** an attractive moorland village whose inn is owned by the local parish council. The medieval **Marchants Cross** stands ½ mile to the south-east.

To the east of Meavy lies the 150-acre **Burrator Reservoir**, Plymouth's main source of water. At its foot is the little village of **Sheepstor** whose churchyard is the resting place of three of the famous Brookes, the family which provided Rajahs of Sarawak for more than a hundred years. A road makes the complete circuit of the reservoir's wooded shores providing many delightful views.

The main road continues to Princetown (see page 49). Opposite the turning to the town centre is a rough road leading to the **Whiteworks** disused mine. This is the part of Dartmoor over which Conan Doyle's Hound of the Baskervilles roamed and the views over the wild fells are remarkable.

2. To Tavistock and Okehampton

Follow the route to Yelverton described in the previous excursion but then remain on the A386 instead of keeping right. A mile beyond Yelverton **Horrabridge**, just off the main road, has an old bridge over the River Walkham and a recently renovated weir and salmon leap which is a thrilling sight when the salmon are running. There is some beautiful river scenery in the area, particularly where the Walkham and Tavy meet at **Double Waters,** reached by a path from Bedford Bridge a little farther along the main road.

After a further 2 miles or so a right turn leads to **Whitchurch** where the mainly fifteenth-century church has barrel roofs, a screen carved with birds and some interesting monuments. Edward Eyre, who explored much of Australia in the middle of the nineteenth century, is buried in the churchyard.

Tavistock

Baths.—Heated open-air pool in Bannawell Street.
Bowls.—The Meadows.
Distances.—Launceston, 14 miles; Liskeard, 19; London, 212; Okehampton, 15; Plymouth, 15.
Early Closing.—Wednesday.

Golf.—18-hole course on Whitchurch Down.
Information Bureau.—Kilworthy Hill.
Library.—Bedford Square.
Market Day.—Friday.
Population.—7,620.
Tennis.—The Meadows.

Tavistock is an ancient town set astride the River Tavy. It has been a place of importance for a thousand years since its abbey, of which few remains survive, was founded in 974. The Benedictine Abbots made it an enormously wealthy and powerful establishment. Tavistock became a Stannary town and was a thriving centre of the woollen industry. It held, as it still does, a weekly cattle market. Its annual Goose Fair, on the second Wednesday of October, still attracts visitors from many miles around. The abbey's prosperity came to an end when Henry VIII dissolved the monasteries. Modern Tavistock has been created mainly by the Russells who were the Dukes and Earls of Bedford and received the abbey lands in 1539. They made their own and the town's fortunes from mining enterprises. The Devon Great Consols mine, 4 miles west of Tavistock, was one of the greatest copper mines in the world during the nineteenth century.

The **Church,** which dates mainly from the fifteenth century, has four spacious aisles, the southernmost known as the cloth-workers' aisle having a fine wagon roof with carved bosses. Of the many monuments the most impressive are those to Judge Glanvill and John Fytz. There is a window by William Morris.

Later buildings of interest in the town include the **Guildhall** and the **Bedford Hotel,** both in Gothic style, and the pinnacled **Town Hall** and **Pannier Market** built by one of the Dukes of Bedford in

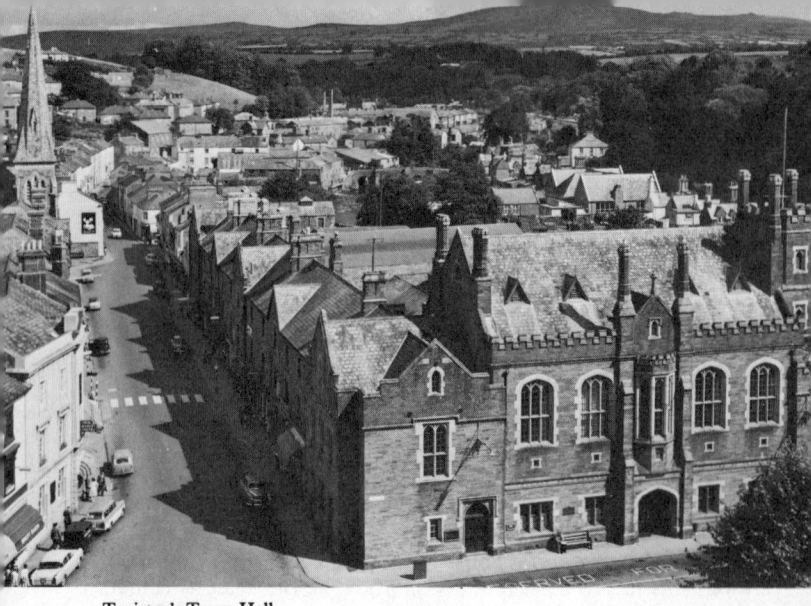

Tavistock Town Hall

the mid-nineteenth century. Where the Plymouth road enters Tavistock a statue stands to Sir Francis Drake who was born in nearby Crowndale.

A most interesting excursion may be undertaken from Tavistock to **Morewellham Quay**, which is reached from the A390 Callington road. This inland harbour was built on the Tamar nearly a thousand years ago for the powerful abbey at Tavistock. The monks exported woollen cloth and tin and imported lime to improve their soil. When the Russell family took over the harbour it soon became one of the most important ports in the west of England, exporting copper, particularly from the Devon Great Consols mine, and also great quantities of arsenic. However by the end of the nineteenth century the port was no longer used and the facilities steadily decayed until in 1970 a trust restored the complex and created a fascinating industrial museum (*all year, daily 10–6, or dusk in winter*). Visitors see an introductory film and tour the harbours, copper chutes, rail tracks, lime kilns and a museum.

The B3357 Ashburton road runs eastward from Tavistock to

Princetown and Two Bridges. The Moor in this area is rich in ancient monuments, particularly near the hamlet of **Merrivale**.

We leave Tavistock by the A386 Okehampton road. In 2 miles a right turn leads to **Peter Tavy**, a picturesque village with a Perpendicular church surrounded by lime trees and with a weather-worn embattled west tower. Back on the main road is the sister village of **Mary Tavy** with a similar church with fifteenth-century wagon roof.

Lydford, to the west of the main road, is well known for its castle, gorge and waterfall. The castle (*open at all times, free*), of which only the keep survives on an artificial mound, was built about 1150 and was used mainly as a prison. The church close by is mainly Perpendicular in style with traces of Early English work. It has an early Norman font, a beautiful piscina and some excellent modern wood carving. For walks and rides in the area, see page 114.

Lydford Gorge (National Trust), a mile west of the main road, lies in a beautifully wooded ravine where the Lyd frets and fumes among great black boulders. The White Lady waterfall has a drop of some 90 feet.

About 3 miles north-west of Lydford just off the A30 at Combebow Bridge stands **Bidlake Mill** (*April to October, Wednesday 2–6*), a medieval corn mill with a water wheel. The rock and water gardens are recent creations.

The A386 continues along the western border of the National Park to Okehampton (see page 44).

4. To Ivybridge

Leave Plymouth by the A38 Ashburton road which skirts the southern borders of Dartmoor. To the south of the road 2 miles out of the city is—

Saltram House
Open Easter to October, daily 11–6; November to March, gardens only open during daylight hours.

This National Trust property stands in a splendidly landscaped park with views extending over Plymouth Sound. The classical façades added in the middle of the eighteenth century hide the remains of a large Tudor house. The interior is notable for fine plasterwork and woodwork, the dining-room and drawing-room both designed by Robert Adam, and a number of Reynolds portraits.

To the north on the A374 is **Plympton**, once a village in its own right but now little more than a continuation of Plymouth. Plympton is famous as the birthplace of Sir Joshua Reynolds. The old Grammar School where he was educated along with companion artists James Northcote, Benjamin Haydon and Charles Eastlake is a seventeenth-century building with a charming cloister. The church is mainly Perpendicular but shows some traces of Early English work and has a fine lofty tower.

In a further 2 miles a left turn leads to **Sparkwell** where the **Dartmoor Wildlife Park** (*daily 10–dusk*) is located. Many species of birds and animals, mainly from Britain and Europe, roam reasonably freely in the 25-acre park.

A road runs north-eastward from Sparkwell to **Cornwood** just inside the National Park. The fifteenth-century church is set by the beautiful valley of the Yealm but the main attraction of the area is the mass of antiquities found on the neighbouring moors particularly on Stall Moor. There are also many ancient farmhouses. A road runs north-westward past china clay works and through fine scenery to Cadover Bridge (see page 86). For a walk in the area see page 124.

The main road continues to **Ivybridge** and in fact by-passes it. Ivybridge lies in a beautiful situation and is a good touring centre for southern Dartmoor.

A road leads northward from Ivybridge to **Harford** situated near many Bronze Age antiquities. John Prideaux, Bishop of Worcester, was born here and in the little Perpendicular church is a memorial erected by him to his parents.

Southward from Ivybridge the B3211 leads in 2 miles to **Ermington**. The church has a thirteenth-century crooked spire and much good wood carving both ancient and modern. To the north-east and reached by the B3210 from Ermington is **Ugborough** which has a surprisingly long church. The screen has 32 painted panels and the ceiling in the north aisle is decorated with extremely interesting carved bosses.

The A38 continues past Ivybridge to South Brent (see page 79).

Walks and Rides on Dartmoor

Introduction

In this part of the *Red Guide to Dartmoor* ten centres have been chosen, or perhaps it would be more accurate to say they have selected themselves. From each of these centres suggested routes are described which taken together give a thorough picture of the best of Dartmoor's scenery. A selection of routes of varied length and difficulty is given. For each route a likely time taken is included, but this will obviously vary as riders may get round the course more quickly—especially if they gallop—and time to stop, stare, take photographs and have a picnic will have to be allowed for.

Because lanes are dangerous to people on horseback the riding routes are on the open moor. Moorland starting points are also more easily reached by "boxed" horses. Riders should not attempt those routes shown as a "walk" as stiles and other physical constraints make them impossible for horses. The Dartmoor National Park Authority publishes a leaflet on riding in the National Park. This, and other informative material, is available from the National Park information centres on the moor or from the Dartmoor National Park headquarters located at Parke, Bovey Tracey.

Access

If the reader follows the descriptions in these pages he will not be guilty of trespass. Dartmoor is a National Park, but this does not mean that it is owned by the nation. The term "National Park" in England and Wales is a planning designation which means that a beautiful area has been earmarked for special protection, and within its boundaries provision is made for the needs of visitors. The land is still privately owned and farmed like any other area of upland, and this situation must be respected by the visitor.

Much of Dartmoor is open country and rough grazing, and large areas are known as commons. A common is a piece of land owned by one person, over which certain people called commoners have rights of grazing, taking stone and turf, and so on, but these privileges do not extend to the public. The fact that land is a common does not automatically mean that the general public has a right of access to it. However, under the National Parks and Access to the Countryside Act there is an assumed right of access, subject to certain standards of conduct, to all land that is wholly or predominantly moor, heath or down. The public is therefore allowed (though not necessarily entitled) to walk or ride over parts of Dartmoor where it has long been accustomed to go, that is, over the commons, the uncultivated enclosures and the moorland part of the Forest (the old name for the central part of Dartmoor).

Threading their way across the moor and winding through the woods and valleys of the enclosed lands are the footpaths and bridleways of the rights of way network. These often possess a fascinating history, having been used by churchmen and drovers, packmen and peat cutters, the miners, and mourners carrying their dead to the parish church for burial. Such humble routes are often muddy and may suffer from bramble snags or the occasional fallen branch until the National Park wardens can get round to clearing the obstruction, but the visitor has as much right to use them as he has to walk along Oxford Street (even though they may pass through crops or farmyards) provided he follows the Country Code. Sometimes these paths are marked by simple signposts, and orange blobs (waymarks) on tree trunks and gate posts act as a reassurance to the walker. These signs are another service provided by the National Park Authority. The routes in this book all use rights of way, or pass over those parts of the moor where access presents no problems.

Precautions

Dartmoor is hill country and makes its own weather. Bad weather is normal, and a beautiful sunny day is, if not unusual, at least something to be remarked upon. This information is not meant to deter the visitor, but to encourage him to dress for the hills, to carry a waterproof, to have a compass, food and drink with him, and generally to be sensible in what he wears. It is not necessary to go to extremes over this (unless the weather is vile, in which case one is wise to stay indoors) but simply to use common sense. This section indicates some of the best routes in the Dartmoor National Park but it is no substitute for a good map. The 1-inch Ordnance Survey

Tourist map is the best one of the area on a single sheet, although the 2½-inch sheets have the edge in matters of detail.

Hazards

The stranger is advised to shun the open moor in mist. However, if overtaken by this all-enshrouding dampness when on his way, he should quickly take stock of the situation and retrace his steps; this is where a compass is called for. Rain on Dartmoor does not often come straight down. If it did an umbrella would be a useful addition to the walker's equipment. Horizontal rain is more frequent. Even waterproofs are not much good in this sort of condition, for the rain drives under the outer layer round the face and trickles down inside, chilling the body. It follows that the Moor is most dangerous to the unprepared when it is wet *and* cold, and in this weather it is best left alone. Dartmoor bogs have a sinister reputation as a result of melo-dramatic references in literature, but they should not give the careful walker or rider any trouble. They betray their presence by a characteristic soft appearance, warning off the observant. Riders should watch carefully where their mounts are treading as it is no easy task to extricate a "stugged" horse.

A great deal of northern Dartmoor (about 27,000 acres) is used by the Services for live firing and other training activities. The bound-aries of the three separate firing areas are marked by red and white posts, and there are notice boards on the main approaches. Poles on high points fly red flags by·day and red lamps by night when firing is in progress, and firing schedules are published in local newspapers on Fridays or may be seen in nearby police stations, post offices and some inns. A telephone-answering service on the following numbers will provide the same information: Torquay 24592; Exeter 70164; Plymouth 701924; Okehampton 2939. The public is allowed to walk or ride over the land used for firing when this is not taking place, but any metal objects lying about should be left untouched.

To get the most out of the Moor the visitor should not worry too much about what might happen to him. Care should nevertheless be taken, and just in case leave a note of your route with someone.

Chagford

Chagford is one of the best centres for walks in the Dartmoor National Park. Radiating from the town are many byways which take the walker through varied countryside. The town itself is well provided with shops, and there are accommodation and catering facilities for every taste within 3 or 4 miles. The open moor is within walking distance and provides a backdrop on the western skyline. What is on the other side of that tor-topped crest, the visitor wants to know. At least one of the walks given here will attempt to answer that question as well as indicate more local strolls nearer the town.

Route 1 (walk)
Nattadon Common
2½ miles—1½ hours
A local walk which includes a steep climb.

Leave Chagford by the road going due south, New Street, which leads off High Street. Turn up left into Nattadon Road, and take the steep path between house numbers 18 and 19 which leads to a stile. Cross a small stream, then follow the steep path with the wall to your left. Near the top of Nattadon leave the path to visit the summit only a few yards away. This is a good place to get one's bearings.

Chagford lies at the foot of the slope to the north, and the nearby hill to the south-west is Meldon Hill. The high land of northern Dartmoor makes the skyline beyond with the rounded form of Cosdon Beacon (incorrectly shown as Cawsand Beacon on maps) the prominent feature halfway to Okehampton. The lumpy rock to the west is Kes Tor, described in Route 3. If visibility is good, Exmoor may be seen many miles to the north. The large building on the end of the spur 2½ miles away to the north-east is Castle Drogo (see Route 2). To the south-east part of Newton Abbot can just be seen through the cleavage of the Bovey valley.

Now rejoin the path and continue to the road. Bracken is sometimes cut here for use as cattle bedding. Turn left at the road and enter the second gate on the right (signposted). The path keeps the hedge on the left until about halfway down when it runs into an old lane which gets very steep near the bottom. On reaching the road, turn left and a short walk brings you back to Chagford.

Route 2 (walk)—Banks of the River Teign to Fingle Bridge by the Fisherman's Path and back by the Hunter's Path
10 miles—7 hours
Some rough parts in the Teign Gorge with a climb to the Hunter's

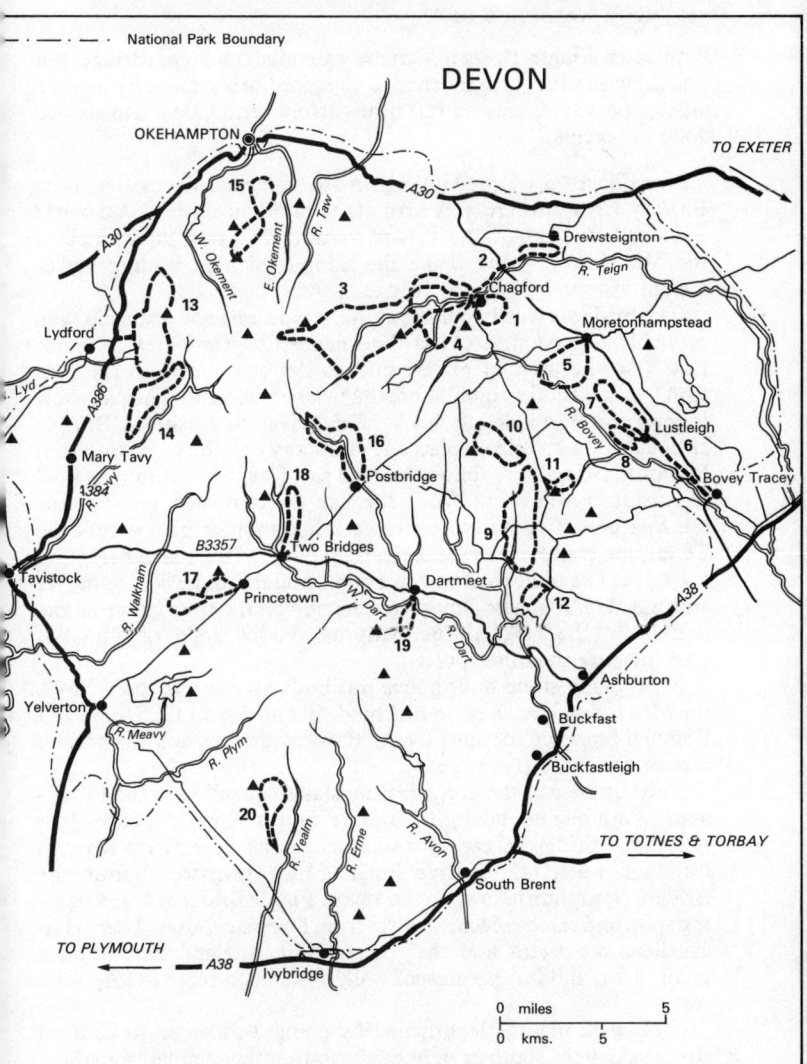

DEVON

National Park Boundary

OKEHAMPTON

TO EXETER

A30

15

W. Okement

E. Okement

R. Taw

A30

Lydford

13

3

2

Drewsteignton

R. Teign

Chagford

1

4

Moretonhampstead

5

7

R. Bovey

Lustleigh

6

A386

R. Lyd

14

Mary Tavy

16

Postbridge

10

11

8

Bovey Tracey

1384

R. W.

18

9

B3357

Two Bridges

Tavistock

17

Princetown

R. Walkham

W. Dart

Dartmeet

12

A38

R. Dart

Yelverton

R. Meavy

19

Ashburton

Buckfast

R. Plym

Buckfastleigh

TO TOTNES & TORBAY

20

R. Yealm

R. Erme

R. Avon

South Brent

TO PLYMOUTH

A38

Ivybridge

| 0 | miles | 5 |
| 0 | kms. | 5 |

Walks and Rides

97

Path after Fingle Bridge. Can be extended to Steps Bridge (on B3212) with the return journey to Chagford being made by bus: 11 miles, one way. Check on bus times before setting out. Can also be done in reverse.

Leave Chagford by the Gidleigh road. The road drops steeply to Factory Cross, where you turn right past the ruins of Chagford Factory, a one-time water-driven woollen mill, now the kennels of the Mid Devon Hunt. Take the signposted path leading downstream just over Chagford Bridge.

The bridge is worth looking at, for it is at least 400 years old, and probably a good deal older. The name Chagford means "gorse ford", so the original place-name no doubt came from the ford which existed at this spot before the bridge was built. The path now follows the north or left bank of the river to Rushford Bridge, although in a couple of places it veers away slightly. Turn left at Rushford Bridge, and follow the road past Chagford swimming pool to Rushford Mill Farm. Walk through the farmyard, pause to see the fine line of stepping stones carrying another path across the Teign, and continue along the riverside path to Dogmarsh Bridge on the A382. Cross the road and carry on through a large field to the far end. Castle Drogo sits almost menacingly on the spur guarding the entrance to the Teign Gorge, with the wooded slopes of Whiddon Park making the other portal.

This totally stone-built house was built between 1910 and 1930 for Mr. Julius Drewe (who had made his money in the Home and Colonial Stores) to designs by Sir Edwin Lutyens, and is a granite *tour de force*. See also page 43.

The entrance to the gorge is unmistakable, and here the Fisherman's Path begins, taking the walker right to Fingle Bridge. Just before the Bridge is reached a weir across the river marks where a leat took water off to drive Fingle Mill, downstream from the Bridge. It was burnt down in the 1890s. Fingle Bridge is an enchanting spot, and can be reached by car from Drewsteignton. There is an excellent restaurant and shop here—The Anglers' Rest—and a picnic area, and for the present walk it is a good place to stop for a rest.

(The walk may be lengthened by going 3 miles on to Clifford Bridge along the south or right bank, and another 3 miles from there

Village inn and church, Drewsteignton

to Steps Bridge on the B3212 from where there are occasional buses to Chagford and Exeter, another restaurant and a Youth Hostel. The riverside stretch from Clifford Bridge to Steps Bridge is on the north bank again and is particularly attractive when the wild daffodils are in bloom in the spring.)

To return to Chagford, turn your back on Fingle Bridge and walk along the road for 200 yards until a signposted path is noticed climbing up through the woods left. Ascend this path, which is a long slog but a pleasant one. If it is summer look for nests of wood ants beside the path. It is therefore unwise to sit down here! At the top a glorious view unfolds. Ahead is northern Dartmoor; the highest land across the valley is crowned by the earthworks of Cranbrook Castle, an Iron Age hill-fort and therefore about 2,000 years old. The path is excellent, and at Sharp Tor (one of ten on the moor) a craggy outcrop enables the walker with a head for heights to look straight down to the river. Castle Drogo is now passed, and just beyond, on the rocky bluff of Hunter's Tor, a steep path through the gorse cuts down to another path near Coombe, a collection of thatched buildings. At the foot of the steep section turn left, and the river is soon reached. The path is now followed upstream back to Chagford.

Route 3 (walk)—Gidleigh, Scorhill, Watern Tor, Hangingstone Hill, Cranmere Pool, Teignhead Bridge, Kes Tor
17 miles—all day
Strenuous, with hard walking, and the likelihood of wet feet in the Cranmere area. Not to be undertaken lightly, but accomplishment gives a feeling of great satisfaction. Check on Services firing programme first.

Follow Route 2 to Chagford Bridge, but after crossing the bridge take the path signposted left. This leads through woods to a steep climb up a field to regain the road at the top. Turn left and pass through the quiet hamlet of Murchington, and 1½ miles on you will reach Gidleigh village cross-roads, a T-junction by the parish hall. Digress here for a few minutes by turning right to view this tiny place.

The church should be visited, and next door are the remains of Gidleigh Castle, a late Norman fortified house which is not open to the public. About 100 yards past the castle gate on the opposite side of the road is Gidleigh Pound, into which small enclosure strays were driven many years ago. The atmosphere of Gidleigh is quite unlike anywhere else; it is as if time has passed it by. There is a Youth Hostel here.

Now return to the T-junction and carry on up the hill (ignoring a turning to the right) to where the road ends at a small car park at the entrance to Scorhill House. Pass through the gate on to the rough ground beyond and follow the left-hand wall. This is Berrydown Stroll, a funnel-shaped arrangement of walls down which animals are driven from the open moor. At the top corner bear slightly left and follow a well-worn track over the top of Scorhill and down the other side.

As you descend, Scorhill Circle is visible on the right. This ring of stones dates from the Bronze Age, say from somewhere between 2000 B.C. and 500 B.C., and is a kind of Dartmoor Stonehenge; a place of religious significance in other words. Return to the track, cross Gidleigh leat by a stone-slab bridge and the Walla Brook by a primitive clapper bridge of venerable but uncertain age.

The way from here is almost due west to Watern Tor, the prominent cockscomb feature on the skyline. It may be necessary to take a course slightly to the north of the direct route to avoid wet ground. At Watern Tor, note Hangingstone Hill with its flagpole away to the south-west, but do not take a direct course as that will lead across the bogs of Watern Combe. Instead take a path which heads for the point where the bowl of the Combe empties its infant stream into the valley falling away to the north. Cross the stream and bear round and up to gain the summit of Hangingstone Hill, at 1,983 feet the third highest point on Dartmoor. There is a Ministry of Defence lookout with a stable for the official's horse as you are within the firing range here. The little building is built against a Bronze Age burial cairn. The hut makes a useful shelter in bad weather. Look around at the view. If the weather is especially clear it is possible to see both the English and Bristol Channels. The two highest points on the moor High Willhays and Yes Tor are away to the north-west. Cranmere Pool is just under 1 mile west-south-west of here across some very rough and wet ground.

The first point to aim for is Taw Head, slightly south of west, and when the tiny Taw is reached follow it to its source in the peaty puddles of the blanket bog. Cranmere Pool is now 700 yards beyond and due west, the intervening ground—a flat peaty plain interspersed with mossy hummocks—being usually wet. The Pool itself is simply a depression in the bog which sometimes contains water, but it is well known as the site of the longest-established unofficial Dartmoor letter box. (There are others now at Fur Tor, Crow Tor, Ducks Pool, and elsewhere.) In 1854 James Perrott, a Dartmoor guide from Chagford, left a bottle in a small cairn so that walkers could leave their visiting cards there. Later it became the custom to leave postcards for the next-comer to post, and in 1905 a visitors' book was added. A well-built stone box acts as the cupboard in which the visitors' book and rubber stamp are stored. The Pool is said to be haunted by Benjie Gear, a swarthy dwarf, the unquiet spirit of a former Mayor of Okehampton.

Now return to Hangingstone Hill. From the summit head south-west aiming for the nearest point of the extensive Fernworthy plantations. On dropping down into the valley towards the North Teign river you will see a large clapper bridge on the right. This used to be the lifeline between Teignhead Farm, the ruins of which are away to the south, and Chagford. Cross the bridge and make for the northern edge of the forest. Now follow it along, heading for the prominent lump of Kes Tor when it becomes visible.

The rock is most easily climbed on the far (east) side. On the top is a fine example of a rock basin. Unbelievably, this round hole in the rock is quite natural, and was formed initially by a small felspar crystal popping-out of the granite, perhaps during a severe frost. The resultant hole filled with water which in turn froze, and so on. Bits of rock fractured and were spun round in the hole by the wind, further weathering and deepening the hole. All this took millions of years. Other examples of this extraordinary process can be seen on the topmost rocks where basins in embryo are being formed at the present time.

Now head for the road visible downhill to the north, passing some broken-down Iron Age walls. Built into them are the ruins of some circular huts—one can easily be picked out by a thorn tree which grows from it. These dwellings had conical roofs thatched with heather or turf. Follow the road off the moor. In about 1 mile take the first turning left after passing through the hamlet of Teigncombe. This is down North Hill Lane, which becomes rough and

Coombe village

steep at the bottom and comes out on a tarmac road at Leigh Bridge where the North and South Teign rivers unite. Carry straight on past the substantial stone house called Holy Street Manor and Chagford is soon reached.

Route 4 (walk)—Yardworthy, Mariners' Way, Gidleigh
10 miles—7 hours
A lane and footpath walk with a few steep hills. Can be very muddy after rain.

Follow the "Fernworthy" road signs from Chagford for 3 miles. About 100 yards short of the cattle grid at Tawton Gate which gives access to the open moor, turn right down Yardworthy Farm lane (signposted). Here the walker joins the so-called Mariners' Way, a reputed foot route for sailors at one time from Bideford to Dartmouth or vice versa. One can certainly postulate a route across eastern Dartmoor, and this is part of it, but whether it ever formed a section of a continuous track right across the county is doubtful. But at all events it is a delightful path to walk, and it is waymarked with orange blobs.

Walk through Yardworthy farmyard and out the other side closing gates as you go. Now keep a hedge on your right and walk downhill and due north through several fields, bearing left for the final drop through trees to a footbridge over the South Teign. Now climb steeply up left to a gate and follow a lane to the road at Frenchbeer. Just before reaching the road the Way passes through the farmyard of Little Frenchbeer (the house has been demolished). By the gate leading into the road is a small stone rectangular building with a barrel roof. This is an ash house, into which the domestic ashes were thrown daily and used later on the fields as fertilizer. This practice was discontinued when artificial fertilizers were introduced. In this part of Devon many ash houses are found with a conical stone roof which sometimes supports a growth of weeds.

Cross the road and enter a path which runs along beneath a cottage with a chimney at the roof apex. The way is clear and contours easily for some distance with stiles in quick succession near Boldventure. These stiles use stone uprights which have probably been doing duty for about 200 years, as can be deduced from the way they have been cut. The method died out at the beginning of the nineteenth century. The path comes out by a farm at Teigncombe and turns left up a rocky lane rejoicing in the name "Featherbed Lane", more properly Teigncombe Common Lane. A short distance up, the Mariners' Way turns right (signposted), meets a short length of road, crosses it, and plunges down into the valley of the North Teign by a waymarked path. The river is crossed by a footbridge at Glassy Steps and then begins the steep climb up to Gidleigh through North Park. At the road turn right and follow the signs back to Chagford. The walker can digress left at the first road junction to see the "village" of Gidleigh (see Route 3).

Moretonhampstead

Moretonhampstead is more of a road centre than a walking centre. But the keen rambler who can read a 2½-inch map will be able to devise his own routes, particularly to the north and east of the town where the land rises to culminate in several small pockets of open moorland at Cranbrook, Butterdon, Willingstone, Mardon, Blackingstone and Pepperdon. See also page 48.

The walk given below heads in the other direction through softly undulating, curlew-calling country.

Route 5 (walk)—Moretonhampstead to North Bovey and back
5 miles—4 hours
This is a summer walk as the field paths are very muddy in winter. There are no very steep hills.

Walk along the Princetown road (Court Street) and turn down the lane (Killerton Lane) just past the last bungalow on the left (signposted). Follow the lane to where it leads into a field where there is a notice board explaining the route from this point. The public right of way goes through Bearland farmyard which is often muddy and involves opening and shutting a lot of gates. A more convenient route using farm tracks has been agreed passing to the south of the buildings and this is well waymarked from here on.

Upon reaching the road bear slightly right, and behind a grassy layby a stile admits the walker to a path which heads for the far corner of the field. Pass through the gate, then turn right through another gate and head for the middle of the opposite hedge. Keep on in the same direction to a stile which brings one out on another road. Turn left and North Bovey is soon reached. The stone wall facing you when you first reach the village is the wall of what was once the village pound.

North Bovey is one of the most attractive villages in Devon with thatched cottages clustered round the tree-shaded green, or Playstow, as it was once called. Many of the trees were planted to mark national events, and these occasions are inscribed on small stones set at the foot of the trees. See also page 48.

From the corner of the green take the road near the Ring of Bells Inn marked "Unsuitable for Motors" and walk downhill passing on to a flat area called Broadymeads through an iron gate. The River Bovey is met here, and there is a footbridge and a fine line of stepping stones. Carry on along the road, turning left at a stone barn. When the lane ends walk along the left-hand side of the hedge, traverse a field, cross a small stream and make for the far top corner of the field. (This path is well waymarked.) Now pass round Fursdon farm through the cattle pens and continue along the lane.

Cross the road and enter the Narramore drive by a large gate. Make for a hidden stile tucked away in the far left corner behind a grove of trees. Follow the path along the bottom hedge of several fields, and it eventually comes out on the road which, by turning right, brings the walker directly to Moretonhampstead.

Bovey Tracey and Lustleigh

Bovey Tracey is just outside the Dartmoor National Park boundary, and is an important local road centre. There are several good hotels and some good shops, including an excellent bookshop. The Dartmoor National Park Authority has established its headquarters at Parke on the B3344 on the edge of the town. See also page 64.

The village of Lustleigh has spread itself over the surrounding hills in an attractive way. Probably no other Dartmoor parish has such a dense network of paths and narrow lanes, and yet it is possible in Lustleigh Cleave to get right away from cars. It is the perfect walking area for close-country rambles; the open moor is a little way away. See also page 64.

Route 6 (walk)—Bovey Tracey to Lustleigh (one way)
3 miles—1½ hours
This walk links these two places, and it is suggested that the return journey should be made by bus.

Leave Bovey Tracey by walking behind the Cromwell Arms and passing through Cromwell's Arch, an object of uncertain origin but certainly older than Cromwell's day. The walk appears to have an unpromising start as you go along a road of Cornish Unit houses to a turning circle at the end, when a cut appears between two of the houses. This leads to a path running along the meadows. It goes to Southbrook Farm and through the farmyard. Take the left-hand gate and follow the edge of the field with the hedge on the right. At the end of the field go through a gate into a wood. That path is now clear and direct all the way to the lane near Wilford Bridge about ¾ mile ahead. The beech woods are splendid in the spring and autumn.

Turn left at the road, go through the old railway track and fork right. Here one enters the National Park. Lustleigh is now about 1½ miles away along this fairly quiet, level country road.

Route 7 (walk)—Lustleigh, Church Path, Sanduck Road and back
3 miles—2 hours
An easy walk with no steep hills. Footpaths out, and back by a quiet country lane

Take the North Bovey road from Lustleigh war memorial, and turn left almost at once along what appears to be a private drive, but a right of way exists for walkers. At the end by a house called "Underwood" turn into a field and follow the path—the Church Path—which contours two fields, and then go along beneath a wood and continue to Lower Combe. Pass the house and go up its approach lane for a short distance, then take the drive to Middle Combe which is also passed on the east side.

The path continues up the valley and presently passes below the gardens of Higher Combe and crosses a stream by a plank bridge. The path comes out into a lane and turns right over a bridge, and immediately left through a gate and into the woods of Sanduck Grove. The path leads to a stony track which the walker should follow uphill to reach the road. Turn right and follow the road back to Lustleigh.

Opposite the Higher Combe drive entrance look over the gate and see the old stone cross standing in the field on its natural rock pedestal. It was placed there in 1860; previously it stood in the bank of the field. The enormous rock beside the road on the hill leading down to Lustleigh is called the Mapstone or the Parson's Brown Loaf.

Route 8 (walk)—Hammerslake, Sharp Tor, Lustleigh Cleave, Heaven's Gate
4 miles—3 hours
Some very steep climbs, wet in places and tall bracken in summer. Glorious views from Sharp Tor and enjoyable footpaths for most of the way.

Follow Route 7—the Church Path—as far as Lower Combe, but turn left here, cross the stream and climb a rough well-waymarked path to the road at Hammerslake. Turn left here, and enter a narrow lane between "Grove" and "North Park".

Passing through a gate at the top of the lane, turn left and follow a path through scrubland which hugs the wall for about 250 yards when another path branches off right and climbs to a small grassy plateau. Several paths meet here, but take the one which leads up the boulder-strewn slope to the north. The climb is steep but short, and brings the walker to the top of Sharp Tor with a splendid view across the valley to Hameldon in the distance. At the bottom of the valley runs the River Bovey, and this slope is the renowned Lustleigh Cleave.

There used to be a natural, delicately-balanced rock here, but it was pitched over the edge not long after the last war by local vandals. So precise was its poise that it could be made to crack nuts—hence its name, the Nutcracker Rock.

Now return to the path by the wall and turn right, following the path around to the left, ignoring all tracks leading off to the right. After 1 mile you rejoin a tarmac road at one of the Lustleigh Cleave access points known as Heaven's Gate, from the scene which met the walker when coming upon it suddenly. Turn right at the road and follow the road signs back to Lustleigh.

Widecombe-in-the-Moor

This famous village was made famous as the result of the popularity of a Devon folk song which speaks about a party of friends from an area north of Dartmoor visiting Widecombe Fair. This event takes place on the second Tuesday in September when enormous crowds descend on the village. See also page 74.

Because it is situated in the valley bottom, the village centre itself is not well placed for walks, so three of the possibilities suggested here involve a short car trip before setting out over the moor.

Route 9 (walk)—Widecombe, Cockingford, and the tors to the east of the Widecombe Valley
8 miles—6 hours
Some road walking at the beginning, and a long climb, but thereafter the walk is mostly pleasant open moor with many tor features and wide-ranging views.

Leave Widecombe by the Dartmeet road and follow it for about 1 mile. Turn left through a green gate marked "Great Dunstone Farm", pass along a lane, turn right into another lane and come out into a field and bear left. Walk through this field and two more, and the path drops down on to the road at Cockingford by a stile. Go past this pretty little hamlet with its old mill and climb the hill keeping straight on at Stone Cross (note the old direction post here) and come out on the open moor at Pudsham Down.

Bear left off the road and make for the top edge of the enclosures. Cross the road coming up from Chittleford and continue north along the outside of the Blackslade enclosures towards Tunhill Rocks. This is a tor in all but name, but is situated on the west side of the hill, and not on the crest. Now climb on to the ridge to the east, making first for Pil Tor and then Top Tor. A mile of easy walking brings you to Bonehill Rocks, and then there is a steep climb past Bell Tor to Chinkwell Tor and Honeybag Tor.

To return to Widecombe, walk down the hill between the last two tors, turn right along the old carriage way, follow it down Thorneyhill Lane to the valley road, then turn left back to the village.

Route 10 (walk or ride)—Grimspound and Hameldon from Natsworthy Gate
3 miles—2 hours, slightly shorter as a ride.
A totally open moor route, starting from just north of Natsworthy Manor (shown on the OS maps) which is 3½ miles north of Widecombe up the valley road, where cars may be left.

Leave the road by the field gate and follow the outside of the plantation wall in a north-westerly direction, heading for a prominent pointed stone on the spur ahead. Soon it disappears from view as the hill is climbed, but presently reappears. It marks the spot where a British bomber crashed in 1941, killing the crew, whose initials are carved on the stone. Carry on up the spur for ½ mile and then bear round to the west along the col between Hameldon Tor and King Tor. Grimspound is in the small, west-facing valley which opens out between Hameldon Tor and Hookney Tor.

Grimspound is a Bronze Age walled village, now ruinous, which was intended to keep stock in and wild animals out. It was not built for defensive purposes. It could have been occupied any time between 1800 B.C. and 550 B.C. The scarred hillside opposite shows where tin has been mined. The small huts inside the enclosure were similar to those described in Route 3. Note how a small stream, the Grimslake, passed through the "village"; however, as a water supply it is unreliable for it dries up in droughts. The question is often asked: "Why did people live right up here in those days?" There are several answers. Much of lowland England was still covered in forests, and as the Bronze Age people needed to pasture their animals grassland was essential. And it is thought that the weather may have been milder. Climate is not a constant factor.

Leave Grimspound by the main entrance and climb south to Hameldon Tor, then strike south-east to pick up the headwaters of the East Webburn where it rises in a small boggy upland combe. There are two boundary stones here. One, the Gray Weather, stands by the upper limit of rushes, and the other, bearing the words Blue Jug, stands by the little stream just before it tumbles over the lip of the combe on its way to the valley to the east. The "DS" on the stones stands for the Duke of Somerset, who was the landowner when the stones were set up. The wooden posts standing to the south were put up in about 1940 to deter enemy aircraft or gliders from landing, or to destroy them if they did. One sometimes sees a pair of red grouse up here. If disturbed they usually take off on a short low flight emitting the call "Go back. Go back. Go back".

Now keep the stream on the right and head back in the direction of the inscribed stone and Natsworthy Gate.

Widecombe and Saddle Tor

Hound Tor

Hay Tor

Route 11 (walk or ride)—Hound Tor and the medieval village site
1 mile—1 hour
An easy short walk or ride. The Hound Tor car park is 4 miles from
Widecombe on the road running north from near the top of Widecombe Hill.

Head for Hound Tor, one of the finest tors on the moor consisting of
several clustered piles of rock. Dartmoor tors are a puzzle even to
geologists, and there are several theories concerning their origin.
Pass through or beside the tor and Grea Tor becomes visible ahead,
and beyond it the Leighon valley with Hay Tor dominating the
skyline.

In the dip between Hound Tor and Grea Tor is the site of the
deserted medieval village excavated in 1961. (If riding, horses can be
tethered to a nearby thorn tree while the ruins are examined.) The
longhouses in which the animals and people lived under one roof
may be seen, the drain at the lower end indicating where the animals
were quartered. Corn was grown, for the corn-drying kilns can still
be seen at the Hound Tor end of the village. The village is thought to
have been deserted about 1350 when the Black Death was on the
rampage, and the present buildings are roughly dateable to
1100–1200. The excavators found evidence of earlier dwellings
going back to Saxon times beneath the stone houses.

Return to the road the same way.

Route 12 (walk or ride)—Buckland Beacon
1 mile—1 hour
A short and very easy route. Make first for Cold East Cross, which is
1½ miles south of Hemsworthy Gate on the Bovey Tracey to Widecombe road. From Cold East Cross go as far as a clump of trees by
the cattle grid, where cars may be left.

Follow the wall around to the south until the small tor which is
Buckland Beacon is reached. The view from this point is one of the
finest on the moor.

The passages of scripture inscribed on the rocks were carved in
1928 by Mr. Clement of Exeter on the instructions of the landowner
Mr. Whitley to mark the rejection of the Revised Prayer Book the
previous year.

Return to the road by the outward route.

Lydford

Lydford is a small village and an enormous parish of about 50,000 acres. The whole of central Dartmoor lies within its boundaries. The village has the starkness of a Cornish settlement as befits its situation on the slopes of western Dartmoor looking across towards Cornwall. The moor rears up beside the A386 and provides numerous opportunities for walks and rides. The routes described here are but two out of many. See also page 91.

Route 13 (walk or ride)—High Down, Doe Tor, Foxhole Mine, Great Links Tor, Peat railway track
7 miles—5 hours
Totally on the open moor, but using tracks where they exist.

Drive up the lane beside the Dartmoor Inn opposite the junction of the road from Lydford with the A386. Leave your vehicle just inside the gate. Cars can be taken across High Down but such random driving does no good to the vegetation and scattered vehicles mar the scenery. The stone cross, made of blocks mortared together, standing on Brat Tor was erected in 1887 to mark the jubilee of Queen Victoria. Follow the wall north-eastward and using the ford or footbridge cross the River Lyd, and take the track contouring south. This is the way the farmer at Doe Tor Farm, one of the more isolated Dartmoor dwellings, used to travel between his home and neighbours, and the ruins of his dwelling are ½ mile from the ford.

As you proceed along this track look across the Lyd to a prominent crag on the west bank with a couple of simple seats in its shade. This is Black Rock, and a plaque records that it was the favourite resting place of a local man who wrote poetry there before he was killed in France in 1918.

From the remains of Doe Tor Farm make up the hill to the east. Riders will pick their way between the tumbled stones. From the summit head north-east to the Doe Tor Brook which should be followed to its source. This small rivulet has been "streamed" for much of its length, that is the stones through which it passes have been turned over for tin-bearing rock. The tumbled heaps represent the spoil—the discarded "dead" rock. Just upstream from where the brook turns through a right angle to flow from east to west are the ruins of a small tin-streamer's house at Foxhole mine. Nearby can be seen two circular buddles beside a small waterwheel pit. Buddles were "dressing floors" where the gravels were sorted by the action of water, and the waterwheel provided power for several processes, one of which was the crushing of the rock. The water was channelled here along a leat, now dry, but discernible above the ruin. The tin dressing process was rather like the gold panning operations one sees in films of the gold rush, but mechanized to the extent that water power did much of the work.

From the head of Doe Tor Brook—a spot known as Dick's Well—make due north for Great Links Tor. Without doubt this is in the top five of Dartmoor tors—some would accord it first place. Now head north-east, and when you have reached the rough metalled track of an old railway turn left, and follow it down. This is the line of the Rattlebrook Head peat railway which wound its way 1,000 feet up from Bridestowe station to the peat workings beyond Great Links Tor. The line was standard gauge, and not surprisingly the peat workings were never a success. The rails were taken up in 1931 but it continued to be worked until 1956 in desultory fashion by a succession of optimistic lessees using road transport.

The sharp angle of a reversing point can be eliminated by cutting across to the lower level, and the track now contours along the west side of Great Nodden, sometimes called Plum Pudding Hill. The Lyd here forms the boundary between the granite and the metamorphic rocks of the border country.

Where the track loops away from the moor cross the Lyd to the east side, follow it downstream and recross it at the original outward crossing point. You are now back where you started from.

Route 14 (walk or ride)—Lanehead, Tavy Cleave, Hare Tor
5 miles—4 hours

A spectacular expedition across the open moor. There is some rough walking across rocky slopes so the rider is given an easier route. Check on the Services firing programme.

From the A386 at Mary Tavy war memorial take the road to Horndon and Willsworthy. At any road junction take the left option and the road ends at a gate giving access to the open moor at Lanehead, ½ mile beyond Willsworthy Farm. Leave the vehicle here.

Follow the farm track right (eastward) towards Nat Tor Farm, leaving the track just before the farm is reached and heading uphill to a bridge over the leat which is easily spotted by the way the animal tracks converge upon it. This leat originally took water from Tavy Cleave to a mining enterprise, but has been adapted to run the turbine at Mary Tavy hydro-electricity station.

At this point the ways of walkers and riders must part. Walkers can take the "low road" into Tavy Cleave along the leat bank, but this will involve too much scrambling for riders who should take the "high road" along the lip of the Cleave. The Cleave is a V-shaped valley along which the Tavy rushes, and the north side of the valley drops theatrically to the river from a rim of crinkly tors. It is along this rim that the rider should go, and his course is described first, in square brackets.

[Riders should cross the leat and make first for Nat Tor, a small cluster of rocks marking the entrance to the Cleave. They should then follow the spur uphill keeping the steep slope on their right. Ger Tor is the next point reached, and then there is a deviation away from the river to circumvent a small side valley. Riders must then return to the Cleave edge at Sharp Tor (Sharp Tor Tavy, to distinguish it from the others on the moor) where the most precipitous drop occurs. Now follow the edge of the slope further north-east until a stream, the Rattle Brook, comes in from the north. At this point the walkers' route will join with that of the riders.]

From the bridge over the leat, walkers should follow the downhill bank "upstream", round the tight curve below Nat Tor. Look out for small trout which flash away as you approach. As you draw near to the leat take-off point where a small building stands, look back and see how the watercourse appears to be flowing uphill—an optical illusion caused by the slope of the land. From the take-off point follow the river up on the same side for $\frac{1}{2}$ mile to the second of two large pools where it is possible to cross to the south bank, but this should not be attempted if the river is running high as it has to be recrossed further up. This second pool is ideal for swimming on a hot day, and has water coming in at the top end down a natural sluice channel. This is where it should be crossed. Now follow the Tavy up to where the Rattle Brook comes in from the north. Walkers should recross the Tavy here. This is where the riders' and the walkers' routes converge.

Trace the Rattle Brook upstream (west bank) for 300 yards or so, at which point a side stream, the Dead Lake, joins it from the west. Follow this stream up to where it is crossed by a track and now make for Hare Tor whose flagpole can be seen on the high land due west.

Hare Tor provides a wonderful viewpoint for the upper Tavy valley, with Fur Tor, the most remote tor, queening it over the solitudes of the central morass. Now head 1½ miles downhill south-westerly and Lanehead is quickly reached.

Okehampton

An important road centre at the northern tip of Dartmoor, and the threshold of numerous walks and rides over the high moor. Good shops, including a walking equipment shop and bookshop. The traveller passing through does not see the best of Okehampton; it needs a leisurely exploration to do it justice. See also page 44.

Route 15 (walk or ride)—Row Tor, West Mil Tor, Yes Tor, High Willhays from Moorgate
6 miles—4½ hours

A rough walk over rocky ground and thick heather to the highest land in the south of England. Some steep climbs. There is no point in attempting this in mist. With so many rough tracks in this part of the moor caused by past and present military activity it is not suggested that riders follow this route as given, but that they devise their own routes in the general area. Check on the Services firing programme first.

Drive up Station Road and Tors Road to the top of the hill above Okehampton. Pass the army camp on your right and leave your vehicle outside the gate near the Moor Brook.

You will have been aware of three prominent tors facing you in line ahead and in ascending order of dominance. These are the three tors given at the head of this route, and Yes Tor is the highest tor on Dartmoor. High Willhays (out of sight from here) at 2,038 feet is 8 feet higher than Yes Tor, but not so impressive as a landscape feature.

With the principal objects in view, a detailed route is hardly necessary, so it is simply suggested that you climb them in the order given above. From Yes Tor walk due south ½ mile to High Willhays to say you have been on the highest land in England south of the

Peak District. For the return, follow one of the tracks back to Okehampton.

Postbridge

Lying on the B3212 between Princetown and Moretonhampstead, Postbridge is a kind of oasis in the middle of the moor which must have been more marked before the extensive afforestation began nearby in the 1930s.

There is a good shop here, some limited accommodation including a Youth Hostel 1 mile away, and a Dartmoor National Park information centre. See also page 49.

Route 16 (walk)—Drift Lane, Powder Mills Leat, Winney's Trough, Sandy Hole Pass, Beehive Hut, Hartland Tor
7½ miles—5 hours
A strenuous walk into the moor, with an easy walk back. Some climbing but nothing severe.

From the large car park at Postbridge cross the twin stiles in the top corner and turn right along Drift Lane, a strip between parallel walls along which cattle were driven (hence the name) from the open moor to the enclosed lands. Follow the track outside the gate bearing left to cross Broad Down Brook. Climb the hill beyond and bear right along the course of a dried up leat. This leat took water from the East Dart river to power the Gunpowder Mills between Postbridge and Two Bridges which ran from 1844 to the 1890s. Follow the leat round and at the take-off point continue up river on the same bank. The East Dart alters direction here and the scenery becomes suddenly dramatic and the walking difficult.

Trace the river upstream to Winney's Trough, the local name for a cataract shown on the map as Waterfall. Cross here and follow the east bank upstream to the narrow defile—Sandy Hole Pass—which is the gateway to the wilderness of Broadamarsh and Cut Hill beyond. The river course where it passes through Sandy Hole Pass has been deepened and the banks walled up. This was done hundreds of years ago by the tin streamers to lower the water level upstream in Broadamarsh so that the tin-bearing gravels could be extracted more easily. This is a good place to picnic and turn round.

Retrace your steps to Winney's Trough, just above which yet

Clapper bridge, Postbridge

another leat was taken off the river in times past. This was—incredibly—8 miles long, and took water to the Vitifer and Birch Tor mining complex near the Warren House Inn. Keep with the leat course round the first hill, then drop down to the East Dart beside the Winney's Down Brook. From here keep with a path which passes through a wall and leads to where the Lade Hill Brook (a corruption of Leat Hill) falls into the East Dart. About 100 yards upstream from here, on the east side of the Lade Hill Brook, are the remains of a small corbelled building known as the beehive hut. Its style is not characteristic of Dartmoor.

Now head due south, climbing slightly on to the ridge to the left and reaching the "back" of Hartland Tor. From here make for the point where the shelter belt ahead meets the river. There is a stile here and a finger post indicates the way along the river bank.

Upon reaching the road, turn right over the road bridge—watch the traffic—and return to the car park. On the way, deviate to view the splendid clapper bridge just downstream. The *Shorter Oxford English Dictionary* quotes an early definition of clapper as "a heap of stones", so this may account for the name on Dartmoor. No date can be given for this bridge.

Princetown

Princetown grew up round the Napoleonic War prison, so has historic interest going back 170 years. Even so, it is not a pretty place, but provides a base for fascinating walks on all sides. There is some accommodation locally, and plenty of in-season catering facilities for the multitudes who come here to experience the strange fascination of seeing the famous prison. See also page 49.

Route 17 (walk or ride)—Old railway track, Swell Tor Quarries, Foggintor Quarries, North Hessary Tor television mast
7 miles—5 hours
An easy walk or ride. Riders will have to dismount to get a proper view of the quarries.

Leave Princetown by the B3212 and once clear of walls and houses make for the line of the old Princetown branch line which is very clear a few hundred yards away to the right. This railway closed in 1956. Follow it for 1½ miles, to where some quarries and ruined buildings become obvious on the right. Ignore these for the time being—they will be visited on the way back. Instead make for the hill to the left of the track. When you get there you will find the far slope has been extensively quarried. These are Swell Tor Quarries. The cutting through which the stone was taken out is very obvious; follow this and it leads to the remains of a siding which eventually joins up with the railway track as it loops round. Just before this junction some huge worked stones will be seen lying around. These were produced for a London Bridge road-widening scheme but were never used.

Now carry on up the railway track as it loops round Kings Tor and back to the first quarries we saw. These are Foggintor Quarries, and are if anything even bigger than the ones at Swell Tor. One hole has a pool and rock climbers use its sheer sides for climbing practice.

To return to Princetown, head up the hill to North Hessary Tor to see the view and the television mast in close-up. When a gale is blowing the noise of the wind in the stays is remarkable. The mast is 750 feet high and was erected in 1954/5. William Crossing, who knew Dartmoor better than anyone before or since, wrote in his *Guide to Dartmoor* in 1909 that one could see sixty tors from its summit, as well as a number of important hills. Now head south to the road on the outskirts of Princetown.

Route 18 (walk or ride)—Two Bridges, Wistman's Wood, Longaford Tor
5 miles—3 hours
An easy walk or ride. Leave your vehicle in the quarry on the east side of the West Dart river at Two Bridges, which is where the B3357 and B3212 intersect in the middle of the moor.

Enter the gate by the quarry and walk north passing the isolated house, Crockern, on your left, and following the orange waymarks through several gates. Once on the open moor these orange blobs are less easy to find, but they guide one to the gate beyond which Wistman's Wood is visible. Just before the gate there are some very ruinous Bronze Age huts on the left.

Wistman's Wood is an oak wood which seems to defy the elements in growing at this height—between 1,300 and 1,400 feet—and in such an exposed site. Many of the trees are gnarled and stunted and bear cloaks of moss and fern, but there is some regeneration going on despite the nibblings of the sheep. A fenced section of the wood is providing Nature Conservancy Council scientists with interesting evidence as to what happens when all grazing animals and human interference are denied. You will see that the vegetation inside the fence is much more vigorous than that outside.

Above the wood, which in addition to oaks contains rowans and hollies, are some long low mounds ranged up and down the slope. These are buries, and were thrown up as artificial warrens for rabbits which were bred here in the last century for flesh and fur.

Climb the hill to the prominent pyramidical tor, Longaford Tor. The summit is easily attained (but not by riders!). Now head south along the ridge. At Littaford Tor, the next large tor along the ridge, go down the hillside to the gate near Wistman's Wood and return to Two Bridges by the outward waymarked route.

Dartmeet

Surely everyone has heard of Dartmeet. That the East and West Dart rivers come together here is overlooked by most visitors, as the actual meeting place is across the road from the car park and almost out of sight.

People come here for the river scenery, to enjoy a cream tea and because they have heard that it is nice. Sheer numbers in the summer often detract from the landscape, but it is still possible to "get away from it all" in a matter of minutes.

Route 19 (walk)—West Dart stepping stones, Combestone Tor
2 miles—1½ hours
A steep climb out, downhill back. The stepping stones at the beginning should not be attempted if they are under water.

From the Dartmeet car park, go over the road bridge—watch the traffic—and notice the ruined clapper bridge just upstream. Go down the signposted path beside the filling station and turn left towards the West Dart river. Cross the stepping stones. The actual meeting place of the East and West Dart rivers is just downstream from here.

Now climb, initially through woods and then fields, finally coming out on the open moor. The right of way is well waymarked

The bridge, Dartmeet

through the enclosures with orange blobs. Make for Combestone Tor, the prominent rock on the hilltop a short distance away. This is the nearest tor on the moor to a road.

If any reader has worked systematically through this guide and walked all the routes he should now feel confident enough to launch out on his own with map and compass. If so, Combestone Tor is a good place to start; the high land of southern Dartmoor is near at hand.

The view from here takes in much of central Dartmoor, from North Hessary Tor in the west to Buckland Beacon in the east, both places mentioned in these route descriptions.

To get back to Dartmeet, return by the outward route.

Cornwood

A curious village, with a mixture of old buildings and less attractive more modern houses. Westwards are the spoil tips of the wide-ranging china clay works, and north are several small wooded valleys running off the high moor. The hill slopes are liberally sprinkled with prehistoric antiquities, but few tors encrust the skyline. See also page 92.

Route 20 (walk)—High House Waste
4 miles—2½ hours

A short easy walk on the southern slopes of the moor. Use your car to get to the starting point from Cornwood. From the centre of the village take the byroad leading towards the moor, then the first left. Follow this narrow winding lane a tortuous mile, ignoring a turning right just after Rook Farm. Leave your car where the road peters out by a stream crossing the road.

Walk up the pleasant track beyond, entering the open moor by a gate—East Rook Gate. There is a grove of tall storm-struck fir trees here which is a prominent landmark for the return walk. Climb the steep slope beyond and bear slightly right. As you reach more level ground covered in dwarf gorse a stream backed by a wall comes into view ahead due north. This is the Ford Brook and marks the western limit of High House Waste. Follow the wall upstream. A gate bears the unusual notice "You are welcome to walk on this land". High House Waste was saved from afforestation in the late 1950s as the result of the intervention of the Dartmoor Preservation Association who now own it and are responsible for the notice. The planted tongue of Dendles Moor across the Broadall Lake to the east shows what the area would have looked like if it had been similarly planted.

Follow the stream and wall up the slope, either inside or outside the wall, and turn right when the wall changes direction. At the highest point stop and look at the view. Two particular features are worth picking out. The mushroom-topped plantation between here and Ivybridge is Hanger Down Clump, and on the skyline of Stalldon, the rounded eminence to the east, you can just pick out the line of tall monoliths comprising the Stalldon stone row, a Bronze Age antiquity of ritualistic significance. Follow the wall down east and where it meets the Broadall Lake there is a cluster of hut circles and enclosing walls which have somehow escaped the later wall builders.

Now contour round to the south. Notice how the wooded nature of the hill slope gradually changes to open moor with altitude. Listen and look for a green woodpecker with its laughing call and undulating flight. The remains of the "High House" are below among the ruined field walls. The place is mentioned in a document of 1781. Leave the Waste by the gate with the notice and head back over the moor to East Rook Gate using the tall fir trees as a beacon. If the weather is clear the Eddystone lighthouse can be picked out to the south-west.

Index